Masala Moments

A travel novel from India

Dorothee Lang

CautionaryTalePress

Akron, Ohio

Fall 2005

Published by Cautionary Tale Press, Akron, Ohio, USA.
www.cautionarytale.com.

Printed in the United States of America.

Cover design and photos by Dorothee Lang.

Shades of their shadows

Their thoughts turning
To masala moments turning
To layers of days

Their souls moving
With the circles of tides
With the flow of sand

The Kochi tree painting
Patterns on square stones
Leading the way

From the gaps of the past
Through the curls of the future
To the now

- Fort Cochin, 2004

Masala Moments

The Key

A long time ago, at the beginning of days, the Gods gathered in the sky, to send life into being. Together, they first created the elements: air and earth, water and fire. Out of them, they formed the world and its continents. Next came the plants and the animals. On the seventh day, they composed mankind.

Finally there was just one thing to be added: the key to wisdom.

"But where shall we put the key," they debated, afraid that mankind would find it before they were ready for it.

"Put it on the highest mountain," the God of the Sea suggested.

"That is not safe enough," said the God of the Clouds.

"Then drown it in the deepest sea," said the God of the Fields.

"You never know the tasks mankind will try to master," the God of Obstacles objected.

So they sat there, searching for the perfect hiding place.

"It won't work like that," the God of Hidden Treasures said in the end. "We have to send a voyager out, to find the perfect sanctuary."

Thus it was done. The voyager was sent, to roam the world, to find the one spot no one would discover.

Weeks went by, months and years, until he finally returned.

"You found the place?" the God of Obstacles asked.

"It took a while, but I found it," the voyager answered. When he pointed at it, the Gods were surprised at first, but soon agreed.

"We should have thought of it before we sent you on that journey," they said.

"No regrets," the voyager replied, and bowed. "It was worth it to travel those roads."

Part 1
In Transit

Walkaway Journeys

The corridor seems grey and endless. June treads through it, towards the plane, towards the long distance connection, all the way to the gate. It is morning still, yet she has crossed mountains already. Has seen the moon set and the sun rise at the same time, above clouds, air born. Has taken the first picture of her journey, unplanned, a sky moment. Now she is down on the ground again. In Milano. Not that it would make a difference.

It isn't open yet, the gate. Two more hours. Time to wait. Time to kill in between movement, time to live in between places. The name for this status: transit. The zone for those who will leave Italy without ever entering it. Just another oddity of life, made comfortable by upholstered chairs armed with massive armrests to keep people from laying down to sleep.

June looks for a free seat. There are three. She takes a moment to figure out the one she will choose. She wants to get things right this time. Right from the start. Not the seat in the first row, with all the people passing directly in front. Not the seat at the edge either, behind the pillar that is blocking the view. The third seat, it will be, the one at the left side. After she finds her place, she reaches for the small black book that is waiting in her bag. Her travel diary. Empty yet, all white. June opens the first page. "Milano," she writes on top of the page, in carefully drawn letters. Now what next, she wonders. She has no clue. So she leaves the entry as it is - a name of a place, uncommented - and takes a look around.

In the seats opposite her, there's a man in a business suit, sleeping. Next to him, a woman wearing dark sunglasses, and her daughter. The girl, dressed all in pink, moves a plastic boat from the bottom of her seat to the top and down again. Up and down goes the boat, down and up, ignoring all laws of gravity.

"She is tired, she has been on the plane all night," explains the mother, as she sees June's curious look.

"Where are you going to?" June asks.

"We are flying home, to the States," the woman explains.

"Home," her daughter echoes, stops the boat where it is, flat at the bottom of the seat, and looks first at her mother, then at June.

"You're ready to go home?" June asks.

The girl keeps staring at her, as if it were a contest, a game show question. Then, instead of answering, she lifts the boat from the seat, and offers it to June.

June doesn't know how to react. She didn't want to play, she just wanted to be polite. But then, you don't get handed a boat every day.

Thus she picks up the toy, turns it carefully in her hands, then offers it to the girl, with the same gesture.

"I have a plane ticket already," June tells her.

"Boat," the girl corrects her. Then, without saying goodbye, she turns around, and loses herself in her game again, sailing the seat, while her mother is reading a book, or at least pretending to do so.

If only I could do the same, zoom out all the others with the snap of a finger, June wishes. She closes her eyes. It doesn't have any effect. The others are there, around her, talking, moving, crossing paths, while a voice announces the last final call for Esa flight 516 to Prague, gate 72. There is music playing somewhere, music without title, elevator music. June tries to concentrate on the tunes, wills herself to doze for a while, to relax.

It works until she hears the footsteps next to her. Someone is leaving. Or is arriving. This won't do, June decides, and opens her eyes again. The girl and her mother are still there. The girl is sitting in the seat now, the mother is reading to her.

"One, two, three, do you know your A, B, C," the mother is reciting, her sunglasses still shading her eyes.

June gets up cautiously; she doesn't want to disturb them. When the girl sees her leave, she turns and waves. June waves back. So they had their goodbye after all, she thinks, as she walks up the corridor she came from. Instead of a quieter place, she finds the book shop she noticed on her way to the gate already. It still isn't open, offering views to the inside, but no way to get there. So she browses the titles from the outside, from a distance. One book draws her attention, "The Walkaway Journey" it is titled.

June hasn't read it, hasn't even heard of it before, yet it wakes memories of another book, of another trip. She can remember neither where she had been back then, nor the book title; but she can still see the image those curled black letters on the page had formed: a place down under, a morning, and all that is left of those who were part of the place for a while, is all that they acquired while they lived there. They left as they came, without explanation, without notice. Had walked away, had walked back home, like summer birds, like winter whales.

Maybe we aren't so different from those aborigines after all, June thinks as she studies the metal birds outside, waiting for their takeoff. Maybe the basic reason for the move she was about to make was as simple as theirs: because it was time for it.

Vegetable Kurma

"Your ticket, please," the flight attendant says, and June shows it once more, there, at the end of the walkway, next to the open door of the plane. Then she is inside, a part of the stream of passengers that floats through the aisles, past the ones that already found their place.

It all seems so organized, June thinks. All those people, all those tickets. All those planes linking to each other. Yet, the truth is: You can never know. Not back home, not here. All you can do is make plans. And then watch things come together or float the other way. Like with this plane. "There might be a strike in Italy," they had said in the news, just a few days before she left. "There might be delays at the airports." June had fished for details on the internet, then called her travel agency. "We heard about that," they had told her, "but the strike isn't definite yet. And even when it happens, you should be fine, as the international flights should be going on time," the man on the service hotline had explained. You should be fine. Better than nothing, but still.

"No guarantees," she had told herself in the morning, when she had shouldered her backpack and closed the door of the apartment she shared with Kathrin and Anna, there in one of the old buildings that form the centre of Freiburg, not far from the Münsterplatz.

At the porch, she had turned around one last time, suppressing the sudden wish to stay here, in the safety net of the everyday, the wish to escape the truth about going, the fact that you can not be sure that you'll return.

The straps of her backpack had felt strangely light on her shoulder when she had walked to the bus station, the very way she had taken so often, on the way to the office. But not today, she had thought, and it was there that she felt this need to leave again, this need to see some other skies, at least for a while, for a few weeks. "I wished I could do the same," Anna had said as she sailed through the door at half past nine, late for the dinner Kathrin had cooked for goodbye, but there at last. "This job is just mad," she had declared, and then opened the bottle of red wine she had brought.

"I'm not sure if the idea of going to India alone sounds exactly that much saner," Kathrin had pointed out once more, but then clinked glasses anyway. "You are still sure you don't want me to drive you to the airport?"

"I will be fine," June had repeated, wishing time would tick either slower, or faster.

Then the morning. The early alarm. The bus to the airport. The sunrise flight over the Alps. There, Italy, and the news that the air strike was postponed, that her plane will be leaving as promised, as hoped for. And now, here, her seat, waiting for her: 23B. Just like her ticket says.

Relieved and excited at the same time, June settles down, and tries to make herself comfortable. She puts the water bottle and her book in the net in front of her, stores the daypack under her seat, buckles the seat belt, and leans back. Done, she tells herself, and peeks out of the window. Nothing is moving yet, but the engines are hissing already. All that is missing now is the start. All that is missing now is saying hello to the one who will sit next to her in the coming hours. She turns.

"Hello," she says.

But the man next to her doesn't react. He is sleeping already.

She notices his tanned skin, his dark hair, and tries to figure out where he is coming from. So close they are, so distant. A stranger a breath away. That's one of the rules of travelling that June always finds odd to deal with: the way personal space is reduced to a minimum while travelling; the way you have to pretend that you're an arm's length away, that you don't feel the other person, so close to you.

A shudder cuts through her reflection. It's the huge body of metal, vibrating. Moving. Its black wheels, starting to turn. Through the window, June can watch the ground pass now.

An hour later, lunch. Below them, it is early afternoon already. That's what the monitor in front says. Local time: 14:35. Time at destination: 18:05. Those two numbers will get closer and closer during their flight towards Asia. The Orient, the land of morning, moving forward in time, while the Occident, the land of the setting sun, moves back in time. And all this without even touching the theory of relativity. Without even touching the laws of time and space. While lunch is getting closer.

Line by line, the stewardess asks the same question. "Vegetable or meat?"

June isn't sure.

"Which kind of vegetable is it?" she wants to know when it is her turn.

The stewardess takes a look at the packs, as if no one ever asked the question before.

"Vegetable kurma," she reads.

"It sounds interesting," June says. "I'll try it."

The stewardess hands her a plate. Lunch is a collection of small square food boxes and plastic cutlery. June opens the main course. Underneath the metal cover, the vegetable kurma: rice, vegetables and a yellow sauce that doesn't taste as spicy as it looks. The dessert, fruit salad.

Outside, islands in an ocean. Maybe Greece, June thinks. The monitor doesn't tell the place. Only the time. As if this was all that mattered.

June turns to the man next to her again, to see if the smell of food woke him from his dreams. But he is still sleeping, and thus, missing the kurma, the islands. Maybe I should try to take a nap, too, now, after lunch, June thinks, and shuts her eyes.

The first thing June sees when she returns from the land of sleep is orange fabric, just a hand from her face. It's clothing, June realizes. It's the shirt of another passenger who is standing in the aisle, here, in the sky, while she has dozed away, for a moment, for how long, she can't say. June keeps her eyes half closed, to linger in this moment in between, when the mind is still in this other place, still arriving, when the positions of inside and outside are still blurry. The humming is there, yet it also could be the echo of the dream that is fading away now, that is losing shape.

Then it's the here, the now, arriving like a visitor. Milano. Her ticket. The start of her journey. What has been a dream itself for a long time, it is happening now. With this thought, June opens her eyes a second time. The inside, the outside. All in place now. The aisle next to her, empty. The humming, coming from the engines. The atmosphere, changing colours, turning towards evening, even here, so high above the ground. June watches the sun rays fade to red and purple, highlighting the horizon. It isn't fading, June tells herself. It's just moving to another place, in an endless circle called day. With this reflection, she turns to the passenger next to her, to the one still sleeping. His head, turning in his dreams, almost resting on her shoulder. His breath touching her skin. And her, feeling comfortable with the closeness. This almost tenderness. I could cross it now, she thinks. Cross the invisible line, just for a second.

The thought, it lingers between them for a moment. The thought, it wakes him up. At least that is how it seems.

"Hi," he whispers when he sees her.

"Hi," she says softly.

For a split moment it seems like they will kiss. Instead, she tells him that he has missed lunch. He tells her that he doesn't mind. His name is Gabino. Or Gavino.

"I am the nomad from Madrid," he explains. "I just travel with myself."

"I am June," she tells him.

"Like the month."

She nods. "Like the month. But I was born in November."

"November," he says, and from the way he pronounces it, almost as if it is was the title of a song, June knows that there is a memory connected for him. There is one connected for me, too, June suddenly figures. That's probably why I am here. Slowly, she turns the thought in her mind, almost amused by it. I have to note this one down, to remember it. But not now, not in the quiet of this moment that unfolded between the humming of the engine, of the voices from the rows in front, and behind them. All those people, she thinks again. All those journeys to all those places. Crossing at one point in time. Her eyes wander back from the rows to the man beside her. He, too, seems lost in thoughts. For a while, they just sit there. Then June picks up the conversation at the very point they left it.

"I was named June because that was the month of the big move. Even before I was born, my parents had the tickets for New Zealand. To a new life," she explains. "Only that it didn't work out. We stayed there for a few years, and then, just when I had finished the first class, my parents split up, and my mother moved back to Germany with me again. You will like it, she promised. *Es wird dir gefallen.*"

"And did you?"

"We returned in winter, and it was freezing cold. One day I walked through town, and there was snow falling, and all was white. I lost all orientation. But I didn't cry, I just kept walking."

"Sounds tough," he says.

"Or stubborn," June comments.

"Maybe those are two faces of the same coin," he suggests, and gestures towards the window, to the shadow clouds outside that could be either dawn or dusk.

"Maybe, from a distance, yes."

"And now?"

"Now I flee the winter instead," she replies. "At least for a while."

He doesn't respond to this. Something about the answer is bothering him, June can see it. "You think I should rather stay?"

"No, not at all," he says. "I just thought that the Maldives would be the more chilled destination. Or the islands of Thailand."

"I know. I've been there," June says. "But this time, I think it has to be India." There is more to that reason, but she leaves it at it. He will understand, won't he, or why else would he be here, in the plane to Mumbai. Or... "Or aren't you going to be travelling there?"

"Yeah, I will," he says, and sighs. "But instead of sights and sounds, it will unfortunately all be about business and projects for me. And most of that, in places no one ever would consider going."

A movie is playing while they talk. Something in black and white. At least that is how June will remember it. A movie about a man, living in a huge city. Trying to make his way out of the wrong part of town, in a time of a recession.

A scene catches their eyes, the man meeting a woman. Some of the lines said, they seem to be included just for them, to fit into their conversation.

"Happiness is a fleeting moment," the man in the film says.

"And sometimes it is a flying moment," the man next to her says. A chocolate bar is his alternate lunch, and he shares it with her, there, above the clouds.

Later he tells her about his dream, to work a few more years, to earn some more of this ridiculous money that comes with this project job. "Just a few more seasons, and then I will go and travel the world," he says, while the man in the movie is standing there, on a bridge, with the woman he met, with the one he can't be with.

"You'll send me a postcard, when you make it?" she asks.

"Yes, I will," he promises.

The film ends there, and they go back to sleep, together this time. They don't exchange addresses, though. They know already that the next day will bring each of them different grounds underneath different skies.

Welcome Goodbye

They go down like an elevator. June's stomach rises the very moment the blue and yellow lights of the runway appear out of nowhere, marking the end of their journey. It's certainly not a movie touchdown. There's no crossing of skylines, no swift last curve, no matching background soundtrack. Yet there they are, unceremoniously dropped from cloudy dreams, even though the display in front states that there are another estimated seven miles to cover. I would like to move through them, June thinks, knowing that it won't be. Instead it's goodbye to Gavino, who's already got his mobile out.

"Back to business," he says. A second later, the mobile starts to ring, confirming his words.

June leans back, and watches the couple on the other side of the aisle make the move she isn't yet ready for. This opening of seat belts. This gathering of things. The man wears a suit in grey colours; his wife wears a sari, the traditional Indian dress. The handbag on her lap matches the colour of her clothes, as do her shoes. She looks as if she just stepped out the door, all fresh, ready for the day. Only that it is the end of the day by now. A part of June admires her for this. She doesn't need a mirror to know that her own appearance is anything but fresh. She shrugs and reaches for her daypack, to get to the comb. That's when the plane comes to a stop.

"Welcome to Mumbai Airport," a voice in the speaker says. "Please open the overhead lockers carefully as items might have shifted during the flight."

Everyone gets up. Jackets are pulled over shirts, over skirts, over blouses. Bags are opened and closed. A queue of passengers starts to form, waiting for the doors to open.

No combing then, June decides, and waves a last goodbye to Gavino, who is standing in the line already, the mobile still squeezed to his ear. She checks the little net in front of her once more. You don't want to lose things before you've even arrived at all.

A door is opened. The queue starts moving. They are there. Outside, it is India. June remains sitting for one more moment. The woman in the sari stands next to her now, putting a shawl around her shoulders. So that is what you wear with a sari, June learns. Not a jacket, but a shawl. She wishes she had one, too, to wrap herself up in. A second skin, warm and comforting, like a cocoon. I will buy one, she thinks. Tomorrow, I will buy one. Then she gets up, takes her daypack, becomes a part of the line, moves towards the door with it.

"Goodbye," the flight attendant says as June steps through the plane door, and gives her the standard smile, a quick movement of the lips, followed by a light nod of the head. An exit sign points toward the left. The corridor that is waiting there has the air of a long tube. There are no windows. There is no visible end. The carpet is green. Dark green. Not the shining green of the sari.

The last corridor she walked through had a plastic floor. Grey plastic. That was in Milano, on the way to this plane. June tries to remember the colour of the carpet in the waiting hall, but there is no picture coming up in her mind. Maybe that is the intention, she thinks. To have an interior architecture so functional that it leaves no traces in the passenger's memory. If it weren't for the green sari, she might have not noticed the colour of this carpet either.

Doors on the side. But they are closed. Leading nowhere. In front of her, a family. A girl in a yellow skirt in the middle, wearing a teddy backpack, holding the hands of her parents, the mother to the right, the father to the left. The girl has to take two steps for each step her parents make. Next to them, a guy with a knitted cap.

I would like to walk this way alone, June realizes. All alone, along this long corridor. That would be a start.

Instead, it's yet another corridor. A walk down a stairway, to another floor. A blue LUGGAGE sign. No carpet here, but stone. No luggage here, either, but another sign. On the parade marches, until it finally reaches the hall with the rotating belt. The first suitcases are already there, arriving in unknown ways, spit out of a black plastic door, to wait for their owners to pick them up.

The family with the girl in the yellow skirt is also here, of course they are. The girl stands there with her mother, while the father is looking for a luggage trolley. June walks off in the other direction, to go to the toilet. Basic needs first. Especially when you have no clue when those needs might be met again.

The airport toilet is at the right end of the luggage hall. June didn't know this, but it somehow seems to fit. She opens the door, expects to find the place empty, as no one has walked towards the door in front of her. But she isn't alone. There is a whole gathering of women in saris, sitting on the floor. In their middle, a small heater. On the heater, a metal pot. Around it, boxes of food. It's midnight lunch break for the staff, or so it seems. June feels like an intruder, but the women just wave at her to come in, and point toward the next room, where the toilets are. Welcome to Mumbai Airport, where things run a little different.

Back at the belt, she waits for the greenish spot of crumpled plastic that is her backpack. One of her fears: to arrive in an unknown place without luggage. To stand there, at the belt, until the end, until all others have picked up their pieces, their suitcases, trolleys, duffle bags, cartons, to see them take the step forward to the belt, picking up their luggage, and walking off, while she is still there. To be the last one, to start the journey without the shirts and trousers she bought for the trip, in light, non-iron fabric, without the medical kit with the tablets for all cases, without the silk sleeping bag that she bought in Thailand and that travelled with her ever since, and without all those other things carefully put together, wrapped up, folded, stored in the belly of the backpack. It had never happened to her, not so far, but she knew it happened too often, you could hear the stories about it, almost everyone seemed to have one, except her. Not this time, she whispers, to no one in particular, to the conveyer belt. Not this time, please. Not in the middle of the night, not here, not now, when all she wants is to get out of the airport, and get to town, to the hotel, to the bed waiting there.

She checks her watch. Eleven-thirty now. If all went well, if all went really well, her luggage arriving soon, no traffic jams outside, the hotel reception open and her room ready, then she would make it at about three o'clock. Which sounded too late. Which wasn't that late, considering the time zone change of three-and-a-half hours. Then it was even early. Apart from the fact that she shouldn't think of this at all, and instead should regard he current time as the only time, and not as a function of home time, and thus, go to bed at the time people go to bed here, and get up at the time people get up here. That's the best way to arrive in a new time zone. Be there.

And it also is the best state for your luggage: be there. And there it is. Moving towards her.

June takes a step forward, picks the backpack from the belt, and places it on the floor in front of her. What next, she wonders. All the time her mind had been waiting for this moment, and now, that it has arrived, and she can walk out of the hall, she feels that she has forgotten something. She looks to the left, to the right. Turns around. Suddenly she feels alone, in between all those people. She remembers a line a friend once had sent to her: "We are all alone, in the crowd."

"Farewell," June whispers, to the others, to all the other strangers. Then she heads to the door that calls itself EXIT. It isn't the real exit yet. Just the exit out of the luggage hall. Next to come: customs. In green and red. SOMETHING TO DECLARE, NOTHING TO DECLARE. June walks through green, through a white door, through another corridor.

Next is immigration, the reason why some passengers suddenly accelerate their steps. A few seconds of speeding up now can add up to the equivalent of minutes saved in the queue to come. Keeping her eyes on the floor, June changes pace, too. On and on and on she overtakes, trying to pretend she has a more valid reason to hurry than the mere fact that she is tired of waiting in queues. All those floors, she thinks. All those procedures. The immigration hall isn't too crowded, though. She walks in zigzags through the walkway formed by plastic poles. Then it's waiting again. Single steps. June peeks to the front desks, but she can't see much yet. This will take a while, she figures. But it doesn't. Suddenly, there is movement. Not single steps, but a whole series of steps. In front, three more desks have opened. Who would expect that, June thinks. A quarter to midnight, and they open immigration desks. Mumbai Airport, things really are different here.

When her turn finally has come, June tries to imitate the standard smile of the flight attendant. "Hello," she says, while she hands her passport to the officer. He just nods, takes the passport, types something into a computer. Maybe her name. Maybe something else. The humming sound of a scanner can be heard. Keys click. The end of the procedure: the sound of ink stamped on paper. The officer hands her the passport. "Thank you," June says, nods once, and stores the passport away. Now she is officially here, walking towards another exit that leads to another corridor. There are counters on both sides. TOURIST INFORMATION, a sign says. The exit can't be far now, even though it is still out of sight.

Walking on, June can feel her stomach curl, wrapping itself up against whatever waits out there. Now she almost wishes for another queue to wait in. But there isn't. June breathes in, checks her luggage one last time, one two three, the big backpack on her back, where it belongs, the small daypack in her hand, the belt bag around her waist, all in place. Breathing out, she starts to walk again, her eyes fixed to the wall at the end of the corridor. She can see herself in a huge mirror hanging on the wall. Underneath it: a row of red plastic chairs. At the ceiling: a green sign, pointing to the right.

The exit is a glass door. June must have crossed some sensor, as it is sliding open already. Behind it: a crowd, waiting, waving at her. She stops to take a look. She hasn't expected so many people. She hasn't expected people at all. Not in the middle of the night. Back home, at this time, airports are deserted places. Not that she would prefer that now. But still. What to do? How to find a taxi now?

Taxi. The word triggers a piece of memory. Isn't there a taxi booth supposed to be here, inside the airport? She reaches for her guidebook, but stops the move in mid-action. First take a few steps back, get out of view, she advises herself, don't make more a fool of yourself than necessary.

Midnight Taxi Downtown

The taxi agent, a bald man in a brown shirt, is waiting for her already. He probably watched her, all the time, watched her as she walked by his booth, as she stood in front of the glass door, as she withdrew and checked her guidebook. His face doesn't tell what he thinks about her.

"Yes, Madam," he says.

"Hello. I need a taxi," June says.

"Yes, Madam. Where do you need to go?"

"To the city," she replies and starts to search her belt-bag for the slip of paper with the address of the hotel. It must be there. She had it in her hands, when she put back her passport. Finally she finds it, and hands it to the man.

"Ah Bentley's," he says. "That is Colaba. Five hundred Rupees."

"Five hundred?"

"Yes, Madam."

She searches for the right note. The first time she pays with Indian money. It feels funny. Five hundred, such a huge note.

The agent takes the money, fills out a form.

"This is your receipt," he explains. "Number 3012."

Then he turns, and points out of the other side of the booth. It's only then that June notices that the booth has windows on both sides, that there are people on the other side, standing there, peeking inside, watching the counter.   The agent points at someone outside, a man in a blue jacket. "When you are outside, give him the receipt," he explains. The man waves at her. She waves back, surprised how well organized everything is. You state the place, they state the rate. You get a receipt with a number. And outside the driver is waiting for you already. Easy enough.

"Thank you," June says, and stores the money and the receipt away. A moment later she remembers that she will need the receipt outside. She opens the bag again, to get it. Okay now, she tells herself. All ready to go. June turns to the glass gate at the front, again. This time she walks straight through, without hesitation. The door closes silently behind her. It is a one-way door, it will not open from the outside.

Outside the air is warm and thick, tasting like smoked incense sticks. "This is me in India," June whispers, breathing in the scent. Then rationality kicks in again. She has to find the taxi driver in this mass of people.

June glances around, and sees that he is there already, just a few steps away, waving at her.

"Hello, Madam, hello. Give me your backpack," he says. She hands it to him, relieved that she doesn't have to carry it herself.

The taxi driver puts one wrist over his shoulder, and starts to walk. June follows through the crowd of people that parts in front of her, to let her through, then swallows her up. They pass some palm trees, their leaves dark shadows above her in the night sky. Then another crowd of people. No cars. Shouldn't the taxi stand be closer, June ponders. Then a thought hits her. What if this wasn't the taxi driver after all, what if the man she just happily handed her backpack to is a thief, specialised in lifting backpacks from arriving travellers? She tries to recall if there was anything written in the guidebook about it. She can't remember.

"Hello, wait a moment," June says, her stomach curling again.

People stare at her, but the man doesn't turn.

"Hello, please wait," she shouts. But her backpack keeps moving away from her. She has no choice but to follow.

Perhaps Kathrin had been right, and coming to India hadn't been such a brilliant idea after all. Perhaps she should have planned the trip better. But again, it was too late for thoughts like this. She was here. Nothing to be done about this now. She shook her head, but couldn't stop herself from imagining tomorrow's headline: "TOURIST FOUND DEAD NEAR MUMBAI AIRPORT."

Wouldn't it be ironic. Travelling so far just to end it all upon arrival. It happens. Life sometimes had it this way. Life sometimes especially had it this way. And on a more rational point, she really was easy prey. She didn't even know where the taxi stand was. How near from the airport, or how far.

Suddenly the man in front of her stops. "Here, Madam. Your taxi."

There it is. A black car. The number on the plate is 3012. It has been there all the time. She has worried for no reason.

The man opens the door for June, and she climbs into the safety of the taxi, feeling grateful to be alive. As simple as that. Her backpack next to her, the hotel reservation in her pocket. Now to the hotel.

But nothing happens. The taxi driver walks away, leaving her alone. Well, not alone, she has to realize just a moment later. A man knocks on the window, to catch her attention.

"Hello, what is your name?" he asks, through the half open window.

"June," she answers, unsure what to make of this.

"Where do you come from?"

"I just arrived," she explains. "And now I want to go to Mumbai, but my taxi driver disappeared."

The man smiles.

"Do you have coins?" he asks.

"Coins?"

"Yes, Euro, Dollar? I am collecting coins."

June doesn't know what to do. Should she give him a coin, would he leave her alone then? She isn't even sure if she wants to be left alone.

"Do you know where my taxi driver has gone?" she asks instead.

"Just a moment," the man says. "Any coins?"

Suddenly someone opens the front door, and gets into the car. It's not the man in the blue jacket. But he has the car keys. Then the man in the blue jacket appears, outside. "Please, Madam," he says.

That's when June finally understands. He never was the taxi driver. He was just the one bringing her to the taxi. Now how much to give him? She has no clue. And she has no change.

"Sorry," she says. "Sorry, no coins."

"But Madam," he protests.

She searches her pockets, finds a 50 cent piece, and hands it to him, hoping it is enough, and not far too much.

The taxi driver turns around.

16

"To what place?" he asks.

"Hotel Bentley's," she explains. "It's in Colaba, do you know it?"

He moves his head slightly, maybe in confirmation, or maybe in thought. Instead of answering, he starts the engine.

June takes it for a yes and eases up. No more questions now for a while. No more decisions to make.

All four windows of the taxi are half open, letting the wind blow through the cabin, letting the air in. June leans back, to relax in the seat, but leaning back won't work. She is too tall for the taxi. She has to lean forward, has to rest her head in her hands to see through the window, to see the world outside, the street formed by huge blocks of houses. Next is a crossing. Traffic lights on each side. Some guys in blue jeans and black t-shirts crossing the street. A jeep standing at a pit stop at the corner, the bonnet open. The traffic light jumps to green, the taxi moves on, towards the city centre. This is India, she reminds herself. It could just as well be Europe, but for the air. She closes her eyes, and the sweet strange taste of India surrounds her, wraps her up like a cloud of scented fog.

The first thing she sees when she opens her eyes again are neon signs. Yamaha. Creating Kando together. Nokia. Get connected. Behind the neon signs, dark houses behind a wall. A strange place, she thinks. Maybe a deserted area. The taxi driver turns to her. "Shanti town," he says, and points into the night. June nods. It takes another minute until she understands. The dark houses, they aren't deserted. They aren't even houses. They are huts. And they are dark, because there is no electricity in the huts. This is a slum. This is advertising for motor bikes and mobile phones in front of cardboard huts. This is India.

Beyond the dark quarter, blocks of buildings again, some of their windows still lit, cubes of life in the night. A Christian church on the right side of the street. A temple on the left side. In the middle, a mile further, another neon sign. "REACH YOUR DESTINATION, NOT YOUR DESTINY," it says.

Another turn, another street. An alley, palm trees on the right side. Beyond it, an empty darkness, as if the city suddenly stopped there. Then a red traffic light coming closer. June waits for the taxi driver to stop, but he doesn't. He drives straight across the intersection. To her surprise, her stomach doesn't seem to mind this at all. She leans back again. The night, the streets, the lights, they form a blur, a river. Just when she wishes for the moment to go on, to last, the taxi slows down in front of a white house.

"Bentley's," the taxi driver says, and opens the door.

"Bentley's Hotel?" she asks.

The driver nods. She looks for a sign, but there is none, at least not above the entrance. The taxi driver sees her look, and points towards a sign at the gate. Bentley's Hotel. Mereweather Road. She is there. Someone from the hotel is already walking her way. Her room is waiting. Easy as that.

Part 2
Mumbai

Inside Streets, Outside Streets

The cry of a bird. Loud and shrill. Or is that a monkey?

June opens her eyes to the rays of light reaching through the window. Outside, it is a new day. She never woke here before, yet it feels strangely normal. Who would have expected that?

The cry again. Curious, she gets up, to peek through the window, to see. And a peek is all she gets. No grand view here, no skyline moment. Just a fragment of the scene. The top of a palm tree, the right part of a roof. Some windows shut. Some windows open. A balcony. But no one there. Not bird, not monkey, not person. Only a solitary chair next to a tiny flower pot. It almost looks like a stage waiting for a performance, like morning rising slowly from the night. Hard to believe it is the same place where she arrived yesterday. Day and night, they are different worlds.

What next? Until this point, her journey was a straight line. The taxi to the airport, the plane to Milano, the stopover there, the plane to Mumbai, the immigration process, the taxi to the hotel, the check in, the room, the bed, the sleep, the waking. One step leading to the next, implicating the next.

It still works like this, June realizes. The sleep, the waking, the breakfast. "For breakfast, you call the room service," the man at the reception had said last night. So she does. Breakfast in bed it will be, for the start. It feels right. She isn't ready to get up, to get out of the room, to get into the day yet, into the outside.

The outside. June reaches for her guidebook. The outside, it is inside the pages, too. She travels the surrounding streets while she sits on the bed. Travels the outside inside her mind. Mereweather Road, Walton Road, Colaba Causeway. In the North, the Fort and Victoria. And in the East, Malabar Hill. On the map, the city seems small. As if you could wander around it in half a day, crossing all those streets, walking back along the Marine Drive to Colaba, along the oceanfront. So it was the sea after all that I saw, in the night, in the taxi, on this palm framed boulevard, June realizes.

A knock on the door brings her back into the room. It's her breakfast, delivered by a young man in a brown suit who is as shy as she is about this procedure. June sits down, pours tea into a miniature tea cup, tastes the toast. Then her mind wanders off again, into the streets.

An hour later, June is out there, for real.

It is warm, hot almost, even though it is still morning. Cautiously, she takes the first steps, but there is no one to be aware of. Mereweather Road is almost empty, except for some cars parked at the side, a man walking by, a dog sleeping in a doorway of an old house that looks like a French mansion. She isn't sure what she expected, but definitely not this atmosphere of timelessness.

Behind the street, a garden. A small park. June remembers having seen it on the map. The gates are closed, but they offer views to the inside, to a water fountain, a circle of ways. She passes the park, then turns left at the next crossing. According to the map, the ocean should be just a street away now, just a few minutes from here. Curious, she walks on. Another street, called Garden Road. More French mansions, their facades telling from other times, leading onwards.

It could be London, June thinks, when a black car is passing.

"Madam, need taxi?" the driver asks.

June shakes her head.

"No, I just want to see the ocean," she says.

The man doesn't respond.

She repeats the last words, adding a question mark to them this time. "The ocean?"

The man stares at her.

Now she wishes she hadn't said the words.

But then the man points toward the end of the road.

So she is right after all.

Another car passes, slows down next to her. June walks on, pretending the car isn't there.

That's how it works, June learns, watching it accelerate again, reaching the corner, and turning to the left. To the ocean. It must be there, just a few steps away now.

And it is, she finds those steps later. The end of the street is the beginning of water. June walks on, to see more, to lean against the stone wall that separates the street from the water.

The ocean. It looks like a lake. No waves, not even the taste of the sea. No breeze, either. Still it is the ocean. So different in places. Reaching from this side of the city to the other side. In her mind, she tries to recall the map of Mumbai. A peninsula on the West coast of India. But the outline doesn't want to come together. So she reaches for her guidebook, wishing it came in parts. To carry all of India in your bag the whole time, the idea suddenly seems odd. Just like this ocean avenue that looks almost forgotten. Strand Road is its name, she sees on the map. The stranded road. How ironic.

June walks along the stone wall, looking for a place to sit, a terrace with a view, a resting spot. There is neither, just like there isn't a beach. Just stones. Down in the water, up there on the side of the road. Stones and sun. So June sits down on the stones. In the distance, a line of ships, red and blue. To the left, buildings. In front of them, a yellow crane boat. From the view, she could be anywhere in the world. Nothing says India here. Not the sights, not the sound.

A minute later, the scene changes.

"Madam, please," someone says, right behind June's back.

June turns, startled by the closeness of the voice. She expects to see an officer, a taxi man. What she sees is a cripple. Crouching on the sidewalk, holding out his thin arm.

"Madam, please," he says again.

June doesn't know what to do. She turns around, irritated, intimidated, hoping he will leave, like the taxi before. She sits there, waiting for a sound. A movement. There is none. At least not outside. Inside, her stomach cringes. She can't keep sitting here; there is no way to keep sitting in this place without knowing what is going on behind her back. She turns around again.

The beggar is still there. At the very same spot. Holding his hand out in the very same gesture.

"Sorry," June says, and moves down from the stones, avoiding his eyes.

"Madam, please," he repeats.

"Sorry," she says again, not knowing what else to say.

Trying to leave her embarrassment behind, June walks on, along the stones, along the ocean. Some street vendors are there, selling peanuts. On the other side of the road, some taxis are parked, their drivers standing next to them, discussing something. June looks around and realizes that she is the only white person in sight. The only stranger. The only woman, too. All the others seem to know the place, know where to go, know what to do.

When she passes the taxi drivers, she wonders what they think of her. This white woman walking along this street. She isn't sure if she really wants to know the answer.

Then June hears it again. The cry that woke her in the morning. Loud and shrill. Right above her head. She looks up, to the roofs, to the tree tops. To the black birds with blue heads. Now she sees them. But they keep their beaks closed.

June waits. Of course, nothing happens.

Move on, she tells herself. The taxi men are probably watching, already joking about you. Move on, and look for a bank, before the banks close for lunch break.

So June walks, into the next street, and the next, passing mansions and trees first. Then she reaches a crowded street that has shops to the left and the right. She passes a window filled with bags, and a stall filled with fruit. There's a blanket on the sidewalk, piles of shoes on it. A cow stands next to it. June steps down on the street, to pass the blanket, the cow. She doesn't want to get too close.

On the other side of the street, June notices a huge tree, its branches reaching from high above down to the ground. Wrapped around its trunk is a coloured piece of fabric. Right in front of it, a woman and three children, sitting there, on the sidewalk stones, cradling a plate of food. A car drives by, honking again and again, even though there is space to drive. Then a group of school children appears, all dressed in the same clothes, white shirt, blue jacket, blue trousers. On some feet, sandals, on other feet, sneakers. June tries not to stare, but it is difficult. There is so much to see. So much she has never seen before.

A bank, June reminds herself. There should be one, here, in this area; June remembers having seen the sign on the miniature map in her guidebook, a dollar sign in the middle of a street. June walks on, past a house plastered with posters, their words printed in a language she can't understand. Then she sees it: a building with tainted windows. BANK OF INDIA, a metal plate says. Bingo, June says, and smiles.

Next to the entry, a man in uniform, carrying a rifle over one shoulder. A guard opens the door for her and points toward a sofa.

"Sit, please," the guard says.

So she sits. On the sofa. And looks at the counters. There are two of them. They are both closed. There is no other customer here in the bank, either. But there is a newspaper, lying on the small table next to the sofa. June picks it up.

"Democracy is not something you believe in or a place to hang your hat, but it's something you do," the quote of the day says. She opens her small diary, to keep the words, this moment. Just when she reached the ending point of the quote, a clerk appears behind the counter.

"Madam, please," the guard at the door says.

June stores the diary away, puts the newspaper back at its place, and crosses the few steps to the counter.

"I want to cash a travellers cheque," she explains, and hands the cheque and her passport to the clerk. What follows is a similar procedure as the one at the immigration desk: keys clicking, a scanner running, more keys clicking, and finally, the sound of ink stamped on paper.

"2225 Rupees," the clerk explains. June stares at the board behind him, the one that lists the exchange rates. *1 Dollar = 45.25* Rupees is noted there, in movable plastic numbers. I should have checked the exchange rate at home, June thinks. There, at the desk, with a calculator, it would have been a matter of minutes to figure out the amount of Rupees she should get for the cheque. True, two thousand something sounded like a lot, yet she had no clue.

"Madam, please sign," the clerk says.

June takes the pen, and tries to concentrate, to do the calculation for herself. Which should be easy enough, unless you have to do it in your mind, in an unknown place. June stares at the paper in front of her. It is filled with numbers and lines. And with blank spaces. One of the blank spaces is for her, to put her name in.

"Two thousand two hundred Rupees," she says to the clerk, half a question, half a statement.

"Yes, Madam," he answers, pointing at the board. "One Dollar is forty five Rupees. Fifty Dollars are two-thousand twenty-five Rupees."

He is right, June has to agree. And what is she scared about anyway. It is not that she is changing money on the street, or in a dubious shack. This is after all, the Bank of India, in the centre of Mumbai.

"Thank you," June says and signs.

The clerk opens another drawer and reaches for an envelope. He puts the money and the receipt inside, and hands it to her. The envelope, against all expectation, isn't white, but yellow, with a blue pattern printed on it.

"It is cute," June hears herself say.

The clerk smiles. He opens the drawer again, and hands her two more envelopes.

June feels like a child. As if transported back in time, to the days when she walked into shops and banks, her hand in the hand of her mother, so that she wouldn't get lost in the new places. Those days when she sometimes received small gifts from the people behind the counter, a slice of cheese in the cheese shop, a plastic piggy box at the bank.

Here, she is that child again, walking into new places she could get lost in, into places where she doesn't know the rules yet. Only that there is no one holding her hand while she makes her way through the day. But then, that is what travelling in India is about, June tells herself. Not a place to hang your hat, but something you do.

Leopold

The gateway to India is an arch, made of yellow stone. A colonial monument that probably rather should be named gateway from India, for the last British regiment marched right through it, before it departed India, that's what she read about it. In front of the arch, a statue of a horseman. And all around it, people.

June walks toward the monument, looking for a spot to sit. To her surprise, there is a free bench. She sits down, and immediately wishes a sombrero, to shade her eyes. The sun is blaring. That's why the bench was free.

A shaded spot, June thinks. That's what I need now. And maybe something to eat. She browses her guidebook, and looks for the pages that list the restaurants in Mumbai.

There is Leopold, she learns, at the corner of Colaba Causeway and Nawroji F Road. Popular with travellers. Next is Bade Miya, on Tulloch Road, an evening street stall. Not the thing for now. Then there is Kailash Parbat, in Sheela Mahal. June reads on, even there is no decision left to make: the first it will be. A traveller place that is just some corners from the Gateway to India, and right on the Causeway, near the Bank of India.

Easy to find, it should be. Only it isn't. June walks past the spot twice until she sees the small sign, dangling from a roof, pointing towards a glass door. Next to the door, glass windows. June peeks inside before she enters, surprised that she hasn't seen it right away. The place is huge; there are more tables than she can count. Yet not one of the tables is free, she discovers once she is inside. Somewhat irritated, June looks around for a place to sit. It's not that she minds sharing a table, it's just that she had this image in mind, that she would be sitting at a corner table, alone, watching people and reading paragraphs from her guidebook while she had lunch. That she would get accustomed to the place slowly without having to interact with anyone but the waiter.

Unsure how to proceed now, June stands there, like a letter delivered but not picked up. Thankfully the dilemma is solved by a woman in an elephant shirt sitting two tables away, who invites June to share her table.

"Thanks," June says, and excuses herself: "It's my first day here."

"No worries," the woman in the elephant shirt says. "It is my last day here."

The woman's name is Kim, and she is from Canada. She has been travelling for five weeks, and is now on the way back to the West, her plane leaving in the night.

"Canada. That's a long way from here."

"It is. The other side of the world. That's why I came here," Kim explains. "I wanted to go somewhere really different."

"Somewhere really different," June repeats. "That's what I came for, too."

The waiter arrives, and June orders rice with vegetables.

"A friend told me to start with light meals," she explains, "even though I feel I should rather order something more Indian."

Kim shakes her head. "You want to start slow. The first day is not the day for experiments."

"So far, my whole day feels like an experiment. Even going to the bank was a little adventure."

"If you want some more of the little adventures, then try one of the cinemas here, and watch a Bollywood movie."

"But it's in Indian, or not?"

"Yes, it's in Hindi, but it's fun. It's more like an opera, with a lot of dance scenes. And the storyline probably will be boy meets girl and they fall in love, even though they aren't supposed to, for there are already wedding plans arranged for them."

"Hindi," June repeats. "That's the language here."

"At least one of them. There are several others. But you will be fine with English, as it's one of the official languages, too."

"But the films aren't in English?"

Kim shakes her head. "Nope. But some of the newspapers and TV channels are."

June nods, and makes a mental note to look for a cinema while she studies the interior of this place, the wooden counter on the right side, the arrangement of plants and flowers in the middle of the room, the photo of New York next to the entrance. She turns around, looking for other photos, and it's then that it happens: a guy with dark hair and an orange vest waves hello. June waves back. The usual hi-you-are-here-too-wave. Then they both turn back to those they are sitting at the table with. Him, to an older man who looks Indian, her to Kim.

"I know him from somewhere," June says. It takes another moment until it hits June. She has no clue who this guy is. Yet she is sure that she has seen him before. The waiter brings her plate, and June looks around again, trying to find the answer. But he is lost in conversation.

"It's probably just someone you saw before in another place. It happens all the time here."

June shakes her head. "But this is my first day here. You are pretty much the first person I have talked to. There is no real *before*."

"I will simply walk over and ask him, when I finish my plate," June decides, still irritated by the incident, and points towards the outside, to change the topic. "Do you have any recommendations for Mumbai?"

"What have you seen so far?"

"Just the area here. I walked along the Strand Road, then went to the bank, and from there to the Gateway of India. And now I am here."

"The thing about Mumbai is, it's really huge. And completely different in places. There is this part here, with all those colonial houses. If you want some really British atmosphere, you could go to Churchgate Train Station. There are cricket places there. It's great to watch for a while. Or you could visit the Hanging Gardens, if you want some quiet and green."

June opens her guidebook, and Kim shows her the places on the map.

"Or you could book a city tour through your guesthouse, that might be the easiest way to get around for the start."

"And where is the airport on this map?"

"It's not on the map. It's further in the North," Kim explains. "Wait, I think it's somewhere on a map in my guidebook."

They look for the airport, and then Kim checks the few lines her guidebook states about languages.

"There are 18 official languages and more than one thousand dialects, it says. And here are some useful words of Hindi: Hello is *namaste*. Yes is *ji ha*, and no is *ji nahi*."

"Namaste. That one I knew already. And what is goodbye?"

"The same: namaste. Then there is thank you: *shukriya*."

"Wait, I will write those down," June says, and takes her travel diary out of her bag. Before she starts to write, she looks to the other table again, though. And to her surprise sees that it is – empty.

"He is gone," she says to Kim. "Now I will never know where we met before."

June stares at the empty table, wishing she had solved the mystery before. Now her mind will keep circling around the question endlessly, unable to find the answer.

"Want to go for a walk?" Kim suggests. "I still need to buy some gifts to bring back home."

"I wanted to buy a shawl," June remembers.

After the air conditioned, relaxed atmosphere of Leopold, the outside feels like a warm loud shock that waited for them right at the doorstep. In a matter of seconds, their skin is covered with humidity, while every step they take is followed by questions.

"Hello, Madam, hello. T-shirt? Watch?"

"Hello, Madam, taxi?"

"No thank you, don't need," Kim says.

"Hello, Madam, hello."

"Hello, Sir, hello," Kim keeps answering, still smiling.

"How long does it take to get used to it?" June wonders.

Kim grins. "No worries, you will get there. Just a few days, then it will be part of you. Or you part of it. However you want to put it."

June shakes her head. The constant rush of voices, of honking traffic, of people addressing her as she passes by seems way beyond any toleration line.

"You know, I miss it already," Kim tells her. "I am ready to go home, and yet I miss it already. Does this make sense?"

They walk on, through the endless crowd of people, then through some side streets. In front of a shop window that is stacked with piles of fabric gleaming in all colours, Kim stops.

"This is a good place to look for shawls. Do you want to have a look?"

June stares at the colours. Some of the patterns feel almost hypnotic. Suddenly, she longs for the quiet of her hotel room. "I think I maybe should have some rest," she says.

So they say goodbye, this different goodbye, the final one. They both know that the chances of ever meeting again are close to zero. Still they exchange their e-mail addresses before they part, before they tell each other to take care, to have a good journey back home, a good journey through India.

Kim steps into the shop, while June dips back into the warm maze of streets. Now she almost finds comfort in the crowd, in the chatter of voices, of sounds, of sights that keep her attention drawn to them. She strolls down the Causeway, looking at those myriads of things that fill the stalls. Books, incense sticks, sun glasses, clocks. Miniature wooden baskets. Plastic plates and cups. And gods. Gods in all sizes, in all forms, with white skin, with blue skin, surrounded by light, by fire, printed on postcards and napkins.

She has no real intention to buy anything. Maybe a little memory of the first day if she came across something. A shirt maybe. A CD. Or a tiny figure, a mascot for her trip. A monkey, maybe. Or a tiger. She starts looking for it, moves from stall to stall, with new interest.

Yet it isn't the mascot June finds. It is the guy she saw in Leopold. He stands there, in front of a shop that sells the Indian version of bongos, waving hello like in a film.

"Hi," June says, stunned.

"Hi," he answers, smiling.

June isn't sure how to proceed. In a movie, this would be the moment the scene turns into a flashback, while the music turns melodramatic. Only that there is no flashback coming up in her brain. No music, either. Not even the slightest piece of recognition.

"We know each other from somewhere," June states.

"Sì," he agrees.

She angles her head, while she squeezes her memory. "I can't remember," she finally confesses.

In a dramatic gesture, he touches his heart with his right hand. When he sees that people are starting to stare, he turns to them, as if this was a theatre, and they are the audience.

"She can't remember me," he exclaims, while June covers her face with her hands.

"Please, I am sorry," she whispers, a sentence that perfectly fits into the show, except that she means it for real.

To June's surprise, the sentence ends the show.

"Don't be sorry," he answers, in a last theatrical move. Then he smiles and shrugs. "I saw you in Milano, in the waiting hall. When I walked past, I thought you were someone else, someone I once met in Barcelona. Later I saw you again in the plane."

That solves the riddle. The plane. She has no real memory of seeing him there, but at some point during the journey their ways must have crossed. That's what made his face look familiar and implacable at the same time.

"And what are we doing now?" June asks, as if there was some kind of protocol for situations like this, and she momentarily forgot about its directions.

"How about going to Chowpatty Beach?"

"Chowpatty Beach?"

"You've never been there? It's really a nice place."

Cups of Chai

The beach. It had been there, all the time. Her only mistake was to look for it on the wrong side of the city. On the right side, beneath the stones, next to the French mansions, a walk away from Mereweather Road. When all the time, it had been here, on the left side, beneath the palm trees, next to this six lane road.

Two other things she learned on the way: the name of the unplaceable one: Jose. And the taxi fare from Colaba Causeway to Chowpatty Beach: 60 Rupees. That is because it is daytime. At night, it would have been 80.

"Palm trees," she says to Jose. "And an ocean promenade. And see, there, a ship coming in."

Jose smiles. "See, I told you it was worth coming here."

He is right, she has to admit it. Still. "It's just that I planned to have a slow start. No sight seeing, no rushing around the place. Stay in the quarter. Get some rest..."

"...and don't climb into rickshaws with a guy you just met at a street corner. And take your umbrella..."

"...and say thank you," she finishes the list.

"Exactly."

"So thanks for getting me to this place."

"It's my pleasure, really."

They walk on, along the beachside. Or rather: they are carried along the beachside in an seemingly unceasing stream of people that flows along the palm framed ocean, along lines of food stalls.

"Fancy a snack?" Jose suggests.

"I am not sure," June answers.

Jose ignores her objections, and hands the man behind the stall two coins.

In return, he gets two little paper rolls.

"Peanuts," he tells her.

"Wrapped in newspaper."

"Yep. Something to read, something to eat. Like they used to sell the fish back home."

On the stones that form the promenade, they find a place to sit. Yet unlike the others, they turn around, from the people passing by to the ocean beyond.

Above them is a huge palm tree, its leaves swaying in the wind. "I think I saw the palm trees through the window of the taxi," June says, "the night I arrived."

"That was this morning then," Jose states.

June has to think twice. But he is right.

"It feels like days ago," she says.

The ocean lies still. It doesn't answer. Neither does Jose. That's how in between the movement, a moment of quiet unfolds, while the voices around them are moulding with the murmur of the waves.

"I wish it was sunset time already," June suddenly says.

"We can stay here until sunset. It's only a few hours."

"I think I need some rest."

"Then you could come here tomorrow."

"It wouldn't be the same."

Jose nods.

"And besides, I will be leaving tomorrow," she adds the more practical reason.

"Tomorrow already?"

This time it's she who nods. "To the South. To the real beaches. I have the ticket already. Booked it from home."

Again they say nothing. It is comfortable. Then she remembers that it probably is her turn to ask about plans. So she does.

"And how about you?"

Jose looks out to the horizon, as if the answer was there. In a way, it is.

"I don't know where I'll go."

She thinks about it. It sounds unexpectedly reasonable, here. "That's a good plan," she says.

Instead of answering, Jose offers her some more peanuts. Again, they sit there munching, watching the horizon, as if it only was a matter of nuts and time until the answer to all questions would appear from a place beyond the water.

Yet it doesn't, and so they return to more practical questions.

"Maybe I'll go to Varanasi again," Jose says, addressing the horizon and June at the same time.

June has no clue what he is talking about. "Varanasi?"

"It's in the North, a holy city at the Ganges River. I visited it on my first trip to India, after some warned me that it would be terribly dirty, and others told me that it is a magic place, and that I had to go there. Thus I said goodbye to the Main Bazaar, packed my bags, and took a rickshaw to the train station, where a night train was leaving in the evening, to arrive in Varanasi in the morning."

"And how was it?"

Jose laughs. "Quite hectic for a holy city. That was one of the first things I thought when I arrived there. Later I learned that Varanasi was only

35

hectic from the outside. Once you made your way to the inner city, and found yourself a room, the place changes. Behind all those streets, beyond all those motion, there is the Ganges, wide like the Nile. And beyond that, nothingness. No buildings on the other side. No bridges leading across the water."

"So I sat, at the river Ganges, and watched the water float by, the boats it carried, and the occasional dead cow. In my hands, a cup of chai, bought from a Sadu, a holy man."

At that point, Jose turns around, and gestures toward a boy that is passing. A second later, he hands June a tiny glass cup, filled with brown liquid.

"What is this?"

"Chai," Jose explains, smiling.

"Chai?"

"That's Hindi. And it means: tea. If you want a cup, you just sit and wait for one of the tea boys to walk by. They are everywhere. And the cups are the same everywhere, too. These small glass cups. Try it, it's good."

"So now we sit here just like you sat in Varanasi?"

"Almost. The atmosphere there is completely different. There are gats along the whole riverside, those stairways that lead to the water. And on one of the steps, there was this café that consisted of nothing but the steps that had always been there, the Sadu's teapot, and some glass cups for the tea. Still, it became my favourite place. It was also the place where I met Julia and Tom, two other travellers, who were coming from Nepal, and heading towards Sri Lanka, where I been a year before. Sitting there, we exchanged travel tales, and sipped tea.

"Then, one day, the Sadu ran out of tea. *Three cups*, we said, like so often before. The Sadu nodded. Then he took his teapot, and walked down the steps. Towards the Ganges. The holy river. Also known as one of the dirtiest rivers of the world. When he reached the water, The Sadu kneeled down. And filled the tea pot with Ganges water. Then he walked up the stairs again, to prepare the tea. When he saw our startled looks, he lifted the teapot, and turned to us. His face angled in reassurance, he pointed at the teapot. *Holy tea,* he explained, enjoying our embarrassment."

June cringes. "You drank Ganges water?"

"Yes. And obviously I survived it. Like they say, it's a holy city."

Sixteen Million Strangers

There are people dancing on Sky Net. There's CNN with the world news. There's a man saying prayers on one channel she can't decipher the name of. There's a program called *No Boundaries No Limits No Rules* on a channel called jeevan. Zebras on National Geographic. June watches them, black and white, in a green-yellow-blue landscape. They've never been to another country, she thinks. They've never seen a map of the world. Never heard the news. For a moment, she finds herself, wanting to be one of them. A zebra in Africa. Living under this vast sky forevermore.

It's ten o'clock. Two hours left in the room. The sight-seeing buses are picking up their passengers now. Not her, though. She had planned to do it, to get on one of those buses today. But then she couldn't make herself get up. It is the second day of the journey, and the jetlag finally got to her. Last night, sleep came in pieces, in parts of hours. There is this feeling of detachment, from the inside, from the outside. There are only three things June can concentrate on at the moment:

That she is holding a ticket for the Konkan Kanya Express that leaves at 22:50 at Chatrapati Train Station.

That she has only two hours left in the room.

And that she isn't ready to check out, to pack the bags and be without a place to retreat to until the evening.

Another day, she thinks. I should have stayed another day. But now it is too late. All is settled. The train ticket is in her pocket, the sight-seeing buses have left. So she stays, here, in this one place that is hers right now, and zaps through the channels of this country. Channel 6 showing *Friends*. MTV India showing pop videos. The same but different. Here, the songs are in Hindi, yet the studios are decorated like the ones in Europe. Two channels further, the same kind of music, yet it is part of a movie that looks like an opera.

June's eyes watch the dancers move in circles, while her thoughts wander back to the day before, to Kim, to Jose, to Chowpatty Beach. In the end, they had stayed at the beach until sunset, had been drifting with the crowd, had some fried snacks here, another cup of chai there. Jose had told her tales of South America, of hikes through the jungle to secret Mayan ruins, and of dinners with members of Bolivian street gangs. At some point she wasn't sure if all those stories really happened to him, or if he just heard them somewhere, picked them up like a bag of peanuts, to spill them in another version, in another place again.

Not that she would have minded it. Still she couldn't resist to make a remark.

"And all this really happened to you? It's unbelievable."

Jose had looked at her, surprised, yet had given her an answer that could be read in either way. "But isn't that the purpose of travelling," he had said, "to give the unbelievable a chance to happen?"

He had a point there, she had to admit it. After all their serial encounters, first at the airport, then in the restaurant, and again at the corner of a city that was inhabited by more than sixteen million people, it was rather against any reasonable odds. Still, it had happened, and in a way it had felt as inevitable as their goodbye at the corner of Leopold.

"Take care," Jose had said, and given her a hug, while she had felt like being in a movie again, and at the same time had tried to fight back unreasonable tears.

"You take care, too," June had answered, wondering if their ways would ever cross again. Maybe some day, at a time and in a place she would least expect it, who could say. And maybe they wouldn't even recognize each other.

"And maybe you really should be getting up now," she tells herself. But like a child, she doesn't want to listen, and zaps through the channels again, searching for the zebras, as if finding them would matter, would be a crucial element of the present situation. Of course, they are gone.

With a sigh, she turns off the TV and walks to the door, to read the rules once more. They still say the same. CHECK IN / OUT: 12 NOON. AIR CONDITIONING OPTIONAL: RS 200 EXTRA.

It's the air conditioning that triggers June's next thought. Or rather, the word "optional." She pulls a blouse over her top, slips into her shoes, and walks down the steps to the reception.

"Yes, Madam," the man at the reception says to her.

"I am leaving to Goa this evening, on a night train," June explains.

"You need a taxi to the train station?"

"Yes, I will need a taxi, but the main question I have is: would it be possible that I keep my room until the evening?"

Instead of giving an answer, the man opens a book in front of him. The book with room reservations, June concludes. Or the book with the prices. She watches him browse the pages, take a pencil, then close the book again. He will say no, she thinks.

"It would be half a rate extra," he says.

June isn't sure if this answer means yes or no.

"So it is possible?"

"Yes, but it would be half a rate extra," the man repeats.

June pays the extra money, knowing that she should bargain instead. Tomorrow, she thinks, and walks back to the room that is hers now. The moment she closes the door, tiredness overwhelms her like a wave. She draws the curtains, slips out of her clothes, and lies down, for a nap. Sleep, which eluded her in the night, now finds her within minutes and carries her deep into dreamland, to a place that is filled with coloured streets where talking monkeys sip Chai tea out of crystal glasses and flocks of zebras are flying through the sky as if they were birds until it starts to rain. She touches her skin, and it is all wet.

This isn't a dream, she realizes. The water on the skin, it is real. As real as the heat that is pressing onto her. Dazed, June opens her eyes. The water, it is sweat. It is her mistake. She has forgotten to turn on the ventilator. She puts it on, and crawls back into bed. There she lies, and watches the humid air getting whirled in circles by the wings of the ventilator that sways with every turn it makes. Not much, just a little bit. Turn. Sway. Turn. Sway. June gets up once more, to move the control from 3 to 4. Then she lies down again, and watches the ventilator move. Turn. Sway. Turn. Sway. There is something hypnotizing about it. Or maybe it is the warmth. The change in hours. Jetlag it is called, she remembers.

I could lie here all afternoon, June thinks. All afternoon, until it is night. It is tempting. Yet it wouldn't do her good, she knows that much, sleeping the day away, getting up in the evening, messing up her system just a bit more. Plus there is this faint feeling of hunger. That is because I haven't eaten anything since breakfast, she figures.

So she gets up, to get a shower, to get dressed, to get back on the Causeway, this street that is the pulse of this quarter, this street that is constantly filled with motion, with automobiles in all sizes, carrying hundreds of people in both directions simultaneously.

At a crossing, while she waits for the light to turn green, she watches the traffic gather and float away. The black taxis with the yellow roofs. The cars. Same as home, if it weren't for the number plates. The trucks. So different. Pink and red. Decorated like for a parade. Flowers dangling from the top of the windshield. Gods painted above them. And the buildings - modern cubes next to curved villas. She gets out her camera, to take a picture. The moment she stores the camera away and looks up again, the lights are green, and a camel is coming her way. It's the first camel she sees. And she missed it by half a minute.

There will be others, she tells herself, and walks down the street, to Leopold. This time, she opens the glass door and steps into the restaurant without hesitation. This time, there is not only one free table, but three. She picks the one in the corner. The one she wished was free yesterday.

Yet it isn't the same, she discovers soon enough. The table June wished for, the table for herself, it feels too quiet today. She orders some food, the same food. Rice and vegetables. While she waits for the plate to arrive, she watches the other guests, sitting there, at the other tables, sitting far away. No Kim today, no Jose. No familiar face. Just strangers. Only that they seem to be at ease, while she doesn't seem to have it in her to relax like the others, like the three travellers two tables down, the ones who sit there, over their glasses and guidebooks, exchanging stories.

June listens to their conversation while she chews her rice. It's then that she realizes that she hasn't really talked to anyone today. That she needs to talk to someone. Now. So she gets up and walks to their table, with a question that doesn't really matter. Some line to start a conversation.

Yet it doesn't work. She has the timing wrong. They are already packing their things and gesturing for the waiter.

"Sorry, we have to leave," one of the women says.

"I just arrived," June tells them.

"You will be fine," the woman answers.

June nods, feeling like a fool.

Part 3
Goa

The Konkan Kanya Express

It's evening, about ten o'clock, yet the streets of Mumbai are still buzzing with traffic. Flocks of motor bikes and black taxis are racing past crossings, followed by coloured trucks and red buses. In front of a huge gothic building that looks like a cathedral, all traffic comes to a halt, cars park in the second and third lane, to drop passengers. A stream of people flows toward a gate that leads to the cathedral, another stream flows out of it.

June stares at the scene, amazed. "What is this?" she asks.

Her taxi driver adds his vehicle to the cars already lined up in the third lane, and stops the engine.

"No, I don't want to visit," June says. "I just wanted to know what it is."

"Victoria Station," the driver explains.

"But I need to go to Chatrapati Station," she says.

"It's the same. Victoria Station, Chatrapati Station, same same," the driver says, and gets her backpack from the rear.

The cathedral – it is a train station with two names. Who would expect that?

"And the train to Goa, where do I find it?"

"Inside," he explains, and gestures toward the gate.

Another bus drives by while June pays the driver. If it wasn't for the coloured trucks, it could be London, she thinks. The heavily decorated red brick building, the red buses, the black cabs. Maybe it won't be so bad inside. Maybe it will look like the original Victoria station inside, too, with a shopping zone, signs leading to the platforms, dedicated waiting areas.

To her relief, the first thing she sees when she walks through the doors is a huge board where trains, departure times and platforms are listed. Almost like in an airport, it is refreshed every other minute automatically. She reads through the list until she finds the Konkan Kanya Express. DEPARTURE 22.50, states the board. PLATFORM NUMBER 15.

Now all she has to do is to find the platform. And buy a bottle of water and a sandwich. June looks around. There indeed are shops, and signs. Signs she never seen before. CLEANLINESS IS NEXT TO GODLINESS, is what one of the signs says, green on white. Next to it, a blue sign, pointing towards ENQUIRY. Underneath the signs, a line of open counters, under siege by a crowd of people.

June squeezes through the crowd, her right hand on her bag. "Be careful, especially in crowded places," Kim had said to her. "Like in all big cities, there are thieves who are out looking for easy prey. Keep your valuables in a money belt, and always pretend you know where you are going. But then, don't worry too much. If you are just a bit careful, and use common sense, you'll be fine."

You will be fine. Hadn't she heard that before?

Pretending she knows where she is going, June walks on, until she finds a shop that sells sandwiches and water. Then she heads towards the waiting hall, hoping to find a free bench. There isn't. In fact, there aren't any benches at all. Instead, the hall is filled with groups of people who gather in circles on the floor, waiting for their train. Some brought blankets to sit on. But most of the people simply sit on the plain stone floor.

June looks for a free spot, and sits down. Now she is part of the crowd, too, she thinks, while her eyes wander through the hall, from one group to the next. There are business people, traders with bags full of goods, families with children, and some even with grandparents. And there are some men, staring at her. "That's what you have to get used to," Kim had said. "The whole concept of Westerners coming to India to backpack through the country probably seems a bit weird to them, and the top of the oddity must be Western women travelling alone. In their culture, a good family would never let a daughter travel alone. That's why Indian families sometimes will ask if you are okay, and invite you to join their meal. They try to give you some protection."

June tries to shake the looks off her mind, and instead concentrates on drawing the scene. Sitting there on the ground, next to her backpack, the small diary in her left hand, a pencil in her right hand, June almost feels comfortable, and doesn't even notice that there is a group of Indians walking her way. It is only when a shadow falls on the drawing that she looks up, and finds herself surrounded by several people who stare at her. Before she can make a move, the man in front of her asks a question she didn't expect at all: "Are you an artist?"

June shakes her head. "I'm just a traveller," she explains, hoping this wasn't the wrong answer.

The man doesn't react. Like the others, he keeps staring at the small notebook in her hands.

"This is my diary," June says, and opens another page, one that holds a scribble of the Gateway to India.

They look at the drawing, then at her. A woman who stands next to the man takes something out of her handbag. Something black.

That's it, June thinks. Now they will rob me. But the black thing isn't a pistol. It's a camera.

"Can I take a photo, please?" the woman asks.

June is stunned. "A photo?"

The woman raises the camera. "A picture of you and my daughter," she decides. A moment later, a girl dressed like a princess sits in June's lap, her hand holding one of June's fingers, while June holds on to her money belt.

"Smile!" the man says. The camera flashes. The girl runs back to her mother.

"Have a good journey," the woman says. Then they are gone, together with the others, leaving June sitting on the ground, with her small diary. She checks her belongings again, but everything is still there.

Thoughtfully, June adds the words: *Are you an artist?* to the diary page. While she finishes the sketch, she dreams of being part of an exhibition one day, of her photo being taken and printed in a newspaper that finds its way to the woman and her daughter, of them cutting the article out of the newspaper, and placing it on a shelf, next to the train station photo, of them showing it to their friends. "We met her, here, at the train station," they will say. "She didn't want to have her photo taken, said she wasn't an artist, but it was clear to see that she was."

Unrobbed and amused by her fantasy of fame, June closes the diary and tries hard not to break in silly giggles. Instead she tries to use common sense, checks the time, and decides to go looking for a toilet, and then walk to the platform. Maybe the train is already waiting there.

It is. Long and red, it sits at the platform. She looks to the left and the right, but she can see neither beginning nor end, nor does she have a clue where she might find Coach Number 8, the one stated on her ticket. On a whim, she turns to the left, and starts to wander along the train, past square windows, past open doors, through groups of passengers. Everyone seems to be on the search, walking hither and thither, tickets in the one hand, water bottles in the other hand, as if they were swords and shields, tools to fight the way to seats hidden in unnamed coaches. Or maybe she is searching on the wrong side of the train. But no, there it is. Coach Number 8. Right behind Coach Number 4. A paper, taped next to the door, lists the names of the passengers. Her name is on it, just like it should be. When she climbs into the train, she finds it half full already, with more and more people coming in, taking one seat after another.

By the time the train starts to move, there is no free seat left, and the air is filled with chatter. There is no way anyone is going to find sleep here, June is sure of that. Yet, to her surprise, it only takes another hour until the train turns into a night train: seats are turned to berths. Pillows and blankets are handed out by train guards. Beds are made. Teeth are brushed. Water bottles placed in the metal holders next to the beds. Legs are stretched. Lights are turned out. Sleep finds the cabin before they reach the next station. The last thing June sees is a flurry of white and yellow lights, shining through the gap in the red curtains. Then it's darkness.

When she looks out of the window again, later, the curtains have been lifted, and the colours have returned. The train runs across a vast plateau. There are other red trains, too, she can see them fly by in the distance, but they don't matter. It's the plateau that irritates June. She has seen it before, she is sure of that. Yet she can't place it. All she knows is that it's daylight, and that all the berths are empty, that all other passengers are gone. She is the only one remaining in this train that was full when it left the station, when it was night still.

I need to find someone, June thinks. There must be some other passengers somewhere. But the next compartment is void of any traces of life, too. There aren't even empty bottles left. As if no one had been travelling inside it for a long time. A guard, June thinks. I have to find a guard.

She returns to her berth, to take her daypack, to make sure to have it with her, whatever happens. Then she starts to walk along the corridor. When she reaches the door to the next wagon, the plateau outside turns into mountains, and the other trains trail away.

June shakes her head, and opens the door anyway. There's no one there, either. Then, finally, in the third wagon, a train guard, standing with the back to her. Relieved, June walks towards him. Yet, when he turns around, she sees that he is only half human, that he has the body of a man, but the face of an elephant.

"Excuse me," June says to him. "Where are the others?"

The elephant guard doesn't respond.

She tries another question. "Where is this train going to?"

Again, the guard doesn't respond.

One last try, June thinks. "Why am I here?"

Instead of answering, the guard starts to break in deep, gurgling laughter.

That is the tune June wakes up to, there, in the moving Konkan Kanya Express. A dream, she tells herself. It's only been a dream. Yet the memory of the blue plateau, of the elephant guard, of his splashing laughter feels strangely real.

June checks her watch. It's half past three. Cautiously, she turns to the other side, and tries to see through the darkness, into the other berths. Of course, the other passengers are still there. Just like the night. Just like the water bottle, above her, in the metal holder. All is good. Goa, the place of sand and water, the place of lazing in hammocks and walking along beaches is a mere two hours and one taxi ride away. There, her journey would finally begin for real.

Wrong Place, Wrong Time

There is a plastic star dangling from the roof. There is a lonely tree standing in the middle of an empty beach. And there is June, sitting in Camilson's Beach Café, staring out into the blue, trying to figure out her mood.

She came here to breathe in the ocean air. To walk through warm sand. To sit and watch the waves come and go. To be in the right place at the right time. "Benaulim," her guidebook had said, "peaceful and rustic, with guesthouses and small hotels spread over a wide area." It sounded like the very thing she needed, after the flight, the buzz of Mumbai. Nothing that possibly could go wrong.

Maybe that had been the mistake. That she didn't even consider the other option. The one she is sitting in now. Wrong place, wrong time. Yes, there is the beach. Yes, it is warm. Yes, it is supposed to be paradise. Only that it doesn't work. At least not for her. The others, they seem to be a part of it. Lisa with the rastas. Tess and Alan who sat there all afternoon, on those wooden chairs, sipping tea, dreaming of staying here forever, or at least as long as the beach was yet unspoiled. "It's terrible what they did to some of the beaches," they told her, "building all those hotels for those people who don't care about the country, who just come for the sun. But here, the beach is yet unspoiled. You were lucky to come to this place."

"I always thought Goa was a town," June confessed. "I had no idea that it is a whole coast."

"It's both," Alan told her. "It's the name of the region, and the name of a town: Old Goa. In the time of the Portuguese, it was the capital. You can visit it, it's surely worth a day trip."

June stared at the map, at the small black spot that was marked Old Goa, pretending she was interested in the history of that place, that she wasn't part of the unconcerned crowd, of those that only came here for the sun.

Later, Lisa spotted the dolphins at the horizon, the ones June couldn't see even when pointed in the right direction.

"There are three, don't you see?" Lisa said.

No, she couldn't. And it wasn't because she didn't try. June longed to see them. The thought that they were right there, in front of her, and yet she were unable to spot them, it almost tipped her over.

"Their fins, they are black triangles in the water," Lisa explained.

All June saw was blue in long waves.

She went to bed early. The exit from the day: sleep. But it didn't work either, didn't want to come to her. There were only pieces of dreams, slices of sleep, leaving her exhausted, leaving her longing for the return of the day. Lying awake, she remembered the dream of the red trains, and it was only now that it scared her, the idea of being caught in a deserted cabin, the image of the elephant-faced guard who only laughed at her questions.

The scene follows her into the morning, the endless empty plateau, the gurgling laughter, like beacons of bad luck. She has to do something about it, she decides, she has to move, and so she gathers the guidebook and the money belt after breakfast, and walks towards the two streets that form the town centre, to look for a travel agency. Or rather: a travel desk. Any place that sells tickets will do. There has to be one, right? All those who arrive here sooner or later need to leave again, and thus need someone to sell them a ticket.

At the one main crossing, June looks around. There are some food stalls to the left. Some shops that sell shell sculptures and sand paintings, too. A mini-market to the right. Opposite it, a closed bank. Some Indians sit in front of it, watching a woman pass by who balances a basket of fruit on her head. There is no agency sign, though. Maybe it's like with the dolphins, June thinks. They are there, but I am too dull to see them. Or maybe it is this heat.

June decides to try her luck in the mini-market. She buys a bottle of water, and then asks for a place that sells tickets. "Over there, Madam, the house with the green sign," the old man behind the counter tells her. June follows his direction, it brings her back to where she was coming from. Yet there it is, the house with the green sign saying TRAVEL in bold letters. She must have been blind.

Inside the agency, there are calendars on the wall, and pictures of Rome and Auckland, of all cities. June checks her itinerary again, this rough list of places she put together back home, when she planned her trip. She crosses out the circles that mark Mumbai and Benaulim.

"Yes, madam," the woman behind the counters says to her.

"I want to go to Hampi," June says.

There are basically two options, she learns. The train and the bus. The train goes twice a week, leaving in the morning. The bus goes every evening.

June decides to take the train. Leaving the ocean in the morning, getting on the train after breakfast, sitting there, watching the landscape pass by, arriving in a new place in the afternoon. How perfect.

The only problem: there are no free seats left on the Tuesday train. She would have to wait until Friday. June shakes her head.

"Then I'll take the night bus," June says. "The night bus tomorrow. Is that possible?"

The woman picks up a ticket. Seat number 42 will be hers. 170 Rupees, leave at 10 in the evening, arrive at 7 in the morning. Sleeper bus, air conditioning. It sounds okay. Plus she will save a day.

With the ticket in her pocket, and the feeling of having things settled, June walks back to the beach, along the street that is too hot at this time of day. June doesn't care. Today, tomorrow, gone, as easy as that, she thinks. Today, tomorrow, gone, she starts to sing, as she walks along the beach. Whenever she gets close to someone passing, June falls silent, though. She doesn't want anyone to hear her childish lullaby. But the beach does. The beach, it didn't have time to care for June, with all the new people arriving the day before. But now, with the words spoken, the beach recognizes her, and sends out a message in a wave. Or so at least it seems, for just a moment later, the whole situation changes: she runs into Halille.

He is standing there, in the shade of a tree, lost in chatter with the fruit woman, who has placed her basket on the ground, turning it into a mini stall with one move.

Their conversation gets interrupted when June walks by.

"Madame, buy fruit?" the fruit woman says to her, pointing at the basket. "Mango, banana, pineapple?"

June stops for a moment. A slice of fresh pineapple, that would be just the right thing now after the walk in the sun. But there aren't slices to be sold. It is all or nothing. "No, sorry, a whole pineapple is too much for me," she decides.

"Well, if you don't mind, we could share one," Halille says.

Of course June doesn't know Halille's name yet. The introduction happens when they are sitting underneath the tree together, waiting for the pineapple to be peeled, in the professional way of the fruit women. When the pineapple is ready, it looks like a delicate piece of food art, almost too beautiful to be munched.

"But that's what it's there for," Halille says, and hands June the first piece.

When the fruit is finished, they go for a walk along the line the waves drew on the beach. That is where they meet the flower girls: dressed in multi-coloured clothes in all kinds of patterns, their hair decorated with pearls and shells, they walk along the same line of waves, yet into the other direction.

"This is Faye, and this is Nel, they are the sand walkers from Sweden," Halille says, and then turns to June.

"I am June, the shade seeker from Germany," June introduces herself, while her eyes still try to grasp the mix of colours.

Nel sees her look, and smiles. "Somehow this beach made us feel like hippies," she explains, and then moves straight on to practical matters. "Want to join us for some Ginger Tea at the Coconut Huts?" she suggests.

"It might take some time to arrive, but it is worth the waiting," Faye adds.

Of course, they are talking about the tea. Still, they could have also meant the beach, this beach that felt so odd to June when she arrived here, stuck in the sun, strangely unmoving. Or has it all been in her mind?

The Coconut Huts are not far, "just down at the next nook of the beach," as Faye put it, and they are just the thing June needed. A small, cosy place, some wooden tables under bamboo shades, all of them with an ocean view. Sitting there, waiting for the tea, they cover the usual travel ritual. How long have you been here, how long will you stay, where do you come from, where are you going to.

"Only three days at this beach, that isn't long," Nel says.

"I know. But then I only have five weeks for the whole trip," June explains. She pauses, waits for Nel to say something. But Nel waits for her to go on. So she names the real reason:

"The truth is, when I arrived yesterday, I didn't like the place too much. And I had this strange dream before I came here, about going the wrong way. So I went to the travel agency this morning, and arranged a ticket to Hampi."

"How are you getting there?"

"With the night bus. The train was full already."

Nel stares at her, astonished. "The night bus, are you sure?"

"Why, is there something wrong with it? It's a comfort bus, with air conditioning and those flexible seats."

Instead of answering the question, Nel looks at Halille and Faye. None of them says a word.

"Well, that's what they say. You might find that the concept of comfort is – how shall I put it – kind of flexible here sometimes," Halille finally says.

"It is...," Nel starts to say, yet gets interrupted by the waiter, who arrives at their table with a plate. Carefully, he places four glasses on the table, and a jar of honey. To June's surprise, the lemon ginger tea is not brewed with tea bags, but with fresh lemon and ginger bits that are still drifting in the glasses. She catches some of the pieces with the spoon, lifts them up in the air, and lets them drop back into the glass.

"It is different," she says.

"It tastes best when you let it rest just a little longer, and then add some honey to it," Faye explains, and then adds: "You said something about a dream."

June puts the spoon aside. "Yes, the dream. It happened in the night train, and it was about being trapped there, while the train moved on and on. It was scary. When I arrived here, I thought I could wind down. But I couldn't. The dream kept haunting me; it was as if it was telling me I was in the wrong place."

June picks up her spoon again, feeling she has said too much already. "Sorry," she says. "I must sound stupid."

Faye shakes her head. "Not at all. I had the oddest dreams here, too. I think it's just what India does. Sometimes, it's almost like movies."

"That was mine, too. Like a strange movie that started in a real place, and then turned abstract. The thing was, I was all alone in the train. And when I went to look for someone, I run into a figure that was half man, and half elephant."

"Ganesh!" Faye exclaims. "You met Ganesh in your dream? That is great! What did he say?"

"You know him?"

Instead of answering, Faye searches her bag, and with a wide smile, hands June a card that carries the very picture of the figure June met in her dream.

Stunned, June sits there. "How can this be?"

"Practical magic," Nel says, then lifts the secret: "Ganesh is a Hindu God. He is the Bringer of Good Luck, the Remover of Obstacles. You find his pictures in temples, and at house entries. You probably have seen him painted somewhere, and that's how he found his way into your dream."

"I met a Hindu God in my dreams," June whispers. She still can't believe it. Then the irony of the scene strikes her. "And when I met him, I asked, *Why am I here?* And you know what he did? He just started to laugh."

"What else did he do?"

"Nothing. He just stood there, and wasn't really very helpful at all for someone who is supposed to be the solver of problems."

Faye grins. "Oh, he doesn't actually solve the problems for you. He just gives hints, or rather: he tells what it takes to overcome obstacles. See the axe he carries?" she says, pointing at the card. "It's for destroying the evil. And in the other hand, he holds a hook and a noose, that's for drawing close those you love, and to reach out to those who are far. And see the lotus flower and the swastika? They are symbols for spiritual knowledge."

June frowns. A Hindu God carrying a symbol of the Nazi regime? "You're kidding me, right?"

"You mean because of the swastika? It is a symbol of luck, here. A symbol of the sun, of life."

June leans forward, to pick up the card. It is there, all right. The symbol of a totalitarian regime, the symbol of life. An elephant, a God. A bus ticket, a cheap trick.

She takes a sip of the soup that is supposed to be tea, swallows a piece of lemon with the liquid on accident, yet manages to put the glass and the card down without coughing. Then the surrealism of the situation overwhelms her, and she breaks into laughter that goes on even when her eyes are spilling tears.

Time and Space Traders

SEA SUN SAND, promises the restaurant sign. And right it is. The only thing it misses is the fish, but that is part of the next place: SEA FOOD HEAVEN. It could be the name of this part of the beach. Fascinated, June stops in front of one of the chalk boards that advertise the menu: Lobster, tuna, shark, red snapper, kingfish and prawns. And, for all who had too much fish, chicken tandoori and vegetable kurma.

The words bring a smile to June's face. Vegetable kurma, that also was the meal they served on the plane. For a moment she considers going into the restaurant and order it, just for the memory. But it is the afternoon. The tables are empty, the people are at the beach. Not that she would mind eating a warm meal in the middle of the afternoon. But sitting in the restaurant alone would feel odd, especially as she will meet Faye, Nel and Halille for dinner later. So she walks on, past the signs, past the fish, towards the water front that is framed in rainbow colours, in pinks and yellows, greens and blues.

June slows down, and gazes at the scene. Like in a fairytale, she thinks, and once more admires the Indian women dressed in their saris, each and every one of them looking like a princess guarded by men in sparkling white shirts. Seeing them, June feels almost out of place, in her simple trousers and shirt. She moves past the gathering at a distance, wondering which special day it is that makes people dress up this way and come to the beach. Then she remembers. It is Sunday. The day of weekend trips and beach picnics. Amused by her complete loss of timing, she walks past couples and families, past women chatting, past children waving at sailing boats, past fathers taking pictures for the family album.

A few hundred metres further, the beach gets emptier, and June walks up to the waterfront. When she reaches it, she puts her shoes in her daypack, and walks on barefoot. While the waves are playing with her feet, erasing the prints they leave in the sand, her thoughts wander back to the Coconut Huts, to the card Faye had handed her there. "Keep it," she had said, "and note the dream scene on its back." So they stand there now, the three questions:

Where are the others?
Where is this train going to?
Why am I here?

"Okay," June had said. "And what does the dream mean then?"

Faye had replied in yet another question: "Maybe that you are on the way to find the answers?"

I wish I was, June whispers, while she walks on. Then a smile crosses her face, like a ray of sun, like a wave of water. For she knows the answers, at least for this moment. The others, they are somewhere at this beach, too. She is going to meet them later at Camilson's. And she is here because she will be gone tonight. Easy as that.

When she arrives at Camilson's, Faye and Nel aren't there yet. Nor is Halille. Which is a good thing. That way, June has some time for herself. She sits down on the chair underneath the dangling star, in the very spot she sat when she felt so out of place here. There, she opens her small travel diary, to paint the star, the ocean. *Take your time,* she writes underneath the waves, wishing she could return to that moment, start over from there. But if I wouldn't have gone to buy the tickets, then I wouldn't have met Halille, and then the flower girls, she considers, and probably would have spent another miserable day here. Who can say.

June lets the thought sink in while she adds another wave to the ocean. When she looks up, she sees Lisa, coming up from the ocean side, from the real blue.

"You are still there?" Lisa says, "I thought you were leaving today."

"I am," June says, and points at her backpack, standing in a corner behind the counter that also is the reception. "I take the night bus from Margao, after dinner."

"Margao," Lisa repeats. "You have a rickshaw to get there?"

"Not yet. I thought I would just walk up to the crossing, there are usually some waiting."

"Why don't you just ask Sira at the reception to order one, to pick you up here?"

"Because – I haven't thought of it, probably." June gets up, then turns around to Lisa. "Thank you."

"No problem. How about a cup of tea for goodbye?"

"Sounds good."

While they are having tea, Halille arrives, together with Faye and Nel.

"You are already having an aperitif!" Nel accuses them cheerfully, then looks for a chair.

"Or maybe we change tables?" Halille suggests.

Again, it's Lisa who has the idea. "I'll ask Sira to put a table up at the beach. That way, we can have a real sunset dinner."

The beach is just a few steps away, but being there, right in the sand, definitely has a different feel to it. The meal they have, it is simple, yet special, too: red snapper, butter naan, some vegetables to go with it.

"It's delicious," Nel says, and they all agree, and keep talking of meals and of beaches, of places they been, carefully avoiding the subject of leaving, of goodbye. It will reach them soon enough, June knows it, as she peeks at the clock on the wall. But not yet.

"Tell one of your travel stories," she says to Halille, who, like Jose, always seems to have another tale waiting to be aired.

"Another tale. Very well," he says, and scratches his head, pretending he really hadn't that much too say.

"Here's what happened to me in Rajasthan," he finally starts his story. "I did a daytrip with two other travellers through the Shekawati Region. One of them, a rich man, had a taxi and driver, and invited us to join him at breakfast. So we went, and drove through those old towns, looking for *Havelis* – those houses with painted scenes outside.

In one settlement, I think it was Nawalgarh, we stopped for a stroll through town. From our road map, we came to believe that it was a small place, and so we didn't even consider the option that we might not find our taxi and driver again. We wandered through side streets, visited several havelis, then found a place to have lunch, one of those small places the locals go."

Halille closes his eyes, and it seems he's there again, in that place, retrieving memories.

"Thali we had, I remember that now. It was excellent. Stuffed, we got up again, to head to our taxi. Well, it didn't take long to find that we had lost all sense of orientation, that we had, in fact, no clue in which direction to turn."

Here, Halille pauses, to give his audience a chance to grasp the situation.

"And then?" Faye says. "How did you get back?"

"Well, as fate had it, right at that moment a kid walks up, and wants to sell us postcards. We try our best to explain to him that it's not postcards we are looking for, but our taxi. "Follow me," the kid says. We shake our heads, telling him that it is *our* taxi we need to find, not any taxi. Again he just says, "Follow me." And so we did, figuring that as we had no clue where to go, we might as well follow him. And now guess."

"He brought you to a carpet store," Lisa suggests.

"Nope, he didn't – he led us through a maze of streets, and five minutes later, we found ourselves in front of our taxi."

"But how did he know where the taxi was?"

Halille sighs. "Really, I never was able to figure that one out."

"Maybe he saw you arriving," June says, and peeks at the clock again. The minutes, who moved so slow on the first day, are floating now.

Again, it's Faye who picks up her mood. "There is still some time, "she says.

And there is. Time for the sunset, time for a last cup of tea, time to exchange e-mail addresses.

When the rickshaw arrives, the leaving finally takes shape. The last words said, they are, as always, "Take care" and "See you again."

"Yes," June replies, to the others, to the ocean. "See you again."

This time, it's a promise, not only a phrase, even though their paths split at this point, with her heading to the East, while Lisa and Halille are moving to the North. But Faye and Nel will head South in a week, and they have already tossed the idea of meeting up again, at the ocean, in Kochi, a place that isn't more than a name to her right now. Just like Hampi. Or Margao, the place the rickshaw is taking her to now.

A mere half an hour later she is there, dropped in front of the place where the bus is supposed to pick her up: The Metropolitan. Somehow she has imagined it to be a huge public building with glass fronts, or a wide stone stairway. In reality, it is a rundown hotel on a dimly lit street that really isn't the best place to hang around in the night. At least she is not alone, there are some others, waiting next to their suitcases and backpacks, too: a man with glasses and a hat, a couple that looks Irish, a guy with a book in his hand.

"The bus to Hampi?" June asks the couple.

"Yes, that's what we are waiting for, too."

June adds her backpack to the small pile that formed next to the fence. She studies the façade, the street. "It's an odd place," she says.

"I just hope the bus is on time," the Irish woman answers.

"It won't be," her boyfriend responds. "Half an hour delay, that's my guess."

"Half an hour would be all right," the man with the hat comments.

"It would be long enough," the woman says.

The man with the hat doesn't respond.

It doesn't matter. The talk, it is small talk. Or rather: waiting for the bus talk. Junes listens to the lines the others exchange, adds one here and there.

Then a vehicle that rumbles along the side street draws their attention.

"The bus," someone says. All heads turn.

Yet it isn't the bus they are waiting for. Without stopping, it drives by.

June shrugs. Then she sits down on her backpack. It's not exactly what it is made for, but it works well enough. She picks up a pen, glances at the hotel façade again. Then she starts to draw a little sketch of the Metropolitan, and adds some lines.

Sitting at the side of the street
watching windows sip the night
waiting for the night bus...

...and there it arrives. Surprised, June gets up, making a mental note to try this trick again sometime soon, to see if it works in other places as well. Or maybe I should rather save it for times of need, she tells herself, as she walks towards the door.

In the bus, the seat that carries the number 42 is already taken. As seem to be most of the other places. June isn't sure what to do. The man who checks the tickets walks by, and June asks for a sleeping seat. He walks on. That's when she remembers Halille's reaction to the night bus, that the concept of comfortable might differ from her expectations.

Obviously it does.

To her surprise, the ticket man returns after a while, and gestures towards a sleeping booth. It is free. It doesn't carry the number 42, but she surely won't complain about that.

The ride in the bus feels slightly surreal. Just after June managed to doze away, there is an unannounced midnight stop in the middle of nowhere. To pass time, she buys a bag of masala chips, and wanders aimlessly around the stopping place, feeding puppies. She doesn't really feel like talking and is glad when the bus driver signals that it's time to leave.

When June recalls the night in the bus later, she isn't sure if that stop ever really happened, or if it was just a dream. What she definitely remembers, though, is seeing the sun rising over shining sunflower fields, and the shop sign in the town after the sunrise: TIME AND SPACE TRADERS.

Part 4
Hampi

Crossings in a Nutshell

There won't be many rooms. June knows that much already. There will be ruins, temples, restaurants, guesthouses and a river. But there won't be many rooms, someone said at the breakfast stop. It is high season, and a small place.

Nested in her bus seat, she reads through her guidebook again. "There are dozens of basic but adequate lodges in the alleys leading off Hampi Bazaar," it says, and adds: "Across the river, a string of guesthouses cater for those who find even Hampi Bazaar too busy. To get there, take a coracle (Rs 5) from the ghats north of the Viruspaksha Temple. In the monsoon season, when the river is running high, boats may not make the crossing."

Above the piece of text, a map. June tries to figure out where the bus might stop, and how to get to the river from there. It's the place to go, everyone said it. Across the river, that's where the best guesthouses are. The river is easy to find on the map. And as it looks, there is basically one main road in Hampi. It should be doable without getting lost, as long as she doesn't walk off in the wrong direction.

A crossing comes up. To the right, a temple. Hampi, someone says. So then, June thinks, and reaches for her backpack, while she rubs the last hazy layer of sleep out of her eyes, while the engine slows down, and everyone in the bus gets ready to move.

Outside, the air is cold and the place is a circus. Another bus is sitting there already. Taxis honk for attention. Motorbikes drive by. June turns around, looking for the way.

"Postcards, Madam," a boy says to her and holds up a bundle of coloured cards.

"To the river?" she asks.

He studies the postcards in his hands. Then his eyes brighten. "Maps," he says, and hands her a booklet.

"But that is a book," June points out.

"But is map inside," he explains.

And sure enough, there is. An artistic map, printed on the last page, including drawings of palaces and temples.

June can't help but smile. "These aren't exactly the places that offer rooms, I guess," she says, and adds a "Sorry."

She needs to leave, she knows it. Next to her, a rickshaw. A guy who came with the bus, too, is discussing rates with the driver.

"To the river?" she asks him. He blinks. "We could share, if you want," he says. "But we have to wait for my friend."

"Ah, no," June decides and walk off, towards the street, without explanation. Her mind circles around three things. Again and again. First: it's too early. Second: she needs a room. Third: She needs to cross the river.

The moment she walks out of the crowd, out of the bus parking area, her thoughts get clearer. There is the street they came from. To the left, the huge temple she saw from the bus. To the right, a hundred metres away, a gate, and behind it, buildings. A few steps away from her, a rickshaw.

"To the river," June says.

The driver gestures toward the back seat.

"How much?"

"Fifty Rupees."

"Thirty Rupees."

"Forty," he says.

"Okay," June answers, and pushes the backpack on the back seat, and sits down next to it, curious for the place that waits around the corner, tired from the night.

The rickshaw drives down the last hundred metres at the street, to the gate. NO CAR INSIDE, a sign next to the gate states. June watches the rickshaw driver manoeuvre through the gate, greeting the guard that stands there. Obviously they don't count as car.

Beyond the gate, the town suddenly starts. There are houses, people, cows. At the end of the street, a huge temple rises to the sky. That's where the rickshaw is going. Straight towards the temple. In front of it, the driver turns to the right, and enters a small alleyway. Another temple appears, in red and white colours. A turn to the left, and another turn to the right. More houses. And then suddenly, a waterway. And two cows, all white, with pink horns. Looking like they arrived straight from fairyland, with the wrong bus. And now got stranded here, at the side of the water.

June turns around, to get a second look, but the driver is waving for her attention.

"The river," he says.

"We are there already?"

"Yes," he says, and points towards a stone stairway that leads down to the riverside. There, in the water, June can see something that looks like an oversized wooden basket.

"These are the boats?" June asks.

"Yes."

Fairyland, June thinks again and pays. Then she shoulders her backpack and starts to climb down the stone stairs.

At the riverside, the ferrymen are waiting. A younger one, at the boat. His partner, or maybe his father, sits on the steps, and collects the fare, a moderate 10 Rupees for the passage. Five for her, five for her luggage that counts like an extra person.

"And the ferry," June asks. "When will the ferry leave?"

The old man shakes his head. "When it is full," he states the obvious fact that needs no questioning.

It's only then that June sees the two other travellers who sit on the steps. A guy with a Lakers t-shirt, and a woman with long black hair. She walks towards them, thinking of something to say, but then just mumbles "Hi" and sits down next to them, to wait for those to arrive who she thought to have outraced already.

But instead of other travellers, it's two Indians who appear, carrying baskets filled with clothes. The old ferryman gestures toward them, shaking his head again. Time to leave, obviously. Or rather: time to get into the shell. Which is easier than she thought. First the backpack, then her. Just when she thought she found the balance, the young ferryman corrects her.

"Kneel down," he orders. That's the way to get over the river: squatting in this nutshell, trying to keep your feet out of the puddle of water that forms in the middle.

A song from her teenage days starts to play in June's mind. Don't pay the ferryman, don't even fix a price, don't pay the ferryman, until he gets you to the other side.

But then, after coming so far, it would be just ironic to drown in a nutshell. With this thought, the nutshell starts its slow move across the river. The river isn't wide, maybe 20 metres, still it takes a few minutes until they reach the other side. After she climbs out of the boat, June looks around just once, then follows the path that leads up the hill. Time counts, now, she knows it, as she reaches Italy. Or rather: Little Italy, how the first guesthouse, set right at the path, is named. Irritated, June looks for the reception. A woman gestures towards the restaurant that connects to the place. June walks into it, and right to the counter.

"I am looking for a room," she explains.

The man behind the counter shakes his head. "Sorry," he says. "All rooms are taken."

It's not the answer she hoped for, but the one she expected to hear.

"You know of a place that has rooms left?"

He shakes his head a second time.

"Okay, thanks," June says and walks on.

A few metres further, a small crossing. Straight on, there is a decorated gate, and behind it, the entry way to more guesthouses. To the left, a small street, harbouring guesthouses on the one side, and a rice field on the other side. Now, where to go. Where to find a room.

June stands there, looking out to the rice field, a lake of water with green dots in it, in front of stone boulders. Then she turns to the left. The first house she passes is a small restaurant. The next is signed "Raju Guesthouse." A man leans at the door, and watches while June walks along the street.

"You look for a room," he asks.

June nods. It's not too hard to guess this, with the backpack that she carries.

"I have a room," he says.

Now that is news. "You have a room," June repeats, just to make sure she got the words right.

"Yes."

"Can I see it?"

"Just a moment," the man says, and walks into the house.

While he is collecting the key, June takes a closer look at the guesthouse. It's a white building, two storeys high, rather small, maybe hosting ten rooms. But it has its own rooftop restaurant. In front of the house, a stripe of green.

"Come," the guesthouse owner says, and June follows, hoping the room is clean and has a shower. It is. And it has. A clean room with a bed in the middle, a tiny window in one wall and a shower in one corner. A place to sleep. Nothing more, nothing less. After the usual bargaining procedure, it is hers. And after a shower, it finally is time to have a real breakfast.

Sitting in the rooftop restaurant, June looks out to the rice field. It's still early, not even nine o'clock. While she waits for her breakfast to arrive, some travellers appear at the crossing, their backpacks on their shoulders. They stand there and look around, just like June did. And like June, they walk towards the left.

"They will have difficulties finding a room," the guy at the table next to her says.

She looks at the travellers, then at him.

"Jan from Prague," he states his name. "You arrived today," he adds.

"June from Freiburg," she answers. "With the night bus."

"I arrived two days ago. Found a place to stay at the end of this road, in a family house. The room I have is really basic. Just a mattress on the stone floor."

"But it's a room," June says.

Jan moves his head in a gesture of agreement.

Later, June's breakfast arrives, chai and some toast. Jan has *alu gobi*.

"Alu means potato, and gobi is cauliflower," he explains.

June notes the words down on a piece of paper.

"And rice?" she asks.

"I don't know," Jan says, and reaches for his guidebook.

While he tries to find the word, the travellers appear again. Walking back from the end of the road, the backpacks still on their shoulders. June watches them walk by, glad she took the hint on the bus seriously, glad that she found the room. Still, she wishes there were more rooms, a good place to stay for everyone who arrives, even though she knows that this isn't how life works.

From Scratch

The place was once a capital. Half a million people lived here. Five hundred thousand. There were universities. Libraries. Theatres. Hampi was "the seat of re-establishment of Indian culture with a flourish for music, art, sculpture, and literature," protected by seven lines of fortification.

Maybe the stone I am sitting on was a part of one of those walls, June thinks. Now it serves as part of the outer wall of a rice field that shimmers in the sun, a haven for a family of dragonflies.

June closes her eyes, tries to see into the past she just read about. Ancient India, what did it look like with its temples, streets and palaces?

A scene from a movie about Ancient Rome comes up in her mind. That's as close as she gets. To see more of the ruins, she would have to return to the bus parking, and then walk along the street in the other direction, until she reaches the Royal Centre. I could go there now, June considers. Cross Italy again, then the river. Or I could stay in the shade, and read some more. Listen to the dragon flies. It's an easy choice. The ruins won't run away, after all.

June rests at the rice field until the shade is captured by the sun. Then she gets up. If she turned to the right, it would be just a few minutes to her guesthouse. She takes the other way, just to see some more of the area. Another guesthouse appears. Then a small shop, the window filled with biscuits and bottles. Good to know. Next is a larger guesthouse, or rather: a larger garden, seating two rows of wooden huts. Gopi, the place is named. Almost like the name for the potatoes. Gobi, that was. Like the desert.

That's one of the difficulties for June, all those names that carry no meaning. That seem like assemblies of letters. Hampi. Gopi. Anegondi. Shanti. That's another guesthouse, or rather: another group of wooden huts in a garden.

I shouldn't do this, she tells herself, as she walks through the entrance gate, to get a closer look. There will be no free huts, and to see where I would rather stay, but can't, will only bring me down. Still she walks on. And yeah. This would be the place. A beautiful setting, some smaller huts on one side, some bigger huts on the other side. An open view to the river, to fields. A tree in the middle. A ladder leading up to it, to a tree house. Hammocks swinging in the breeze. Music playing somewhere.

June sighs. Not for you, she tells herself. Then she has an idea. All rooms are taken today, yes. But what about tomorrow?

She walks to the reception.

"Is there a free bungalow..." she starts to ask.

"Yes," the man behind the reception answers, before she can add the "tomorrow."

Stunned, she looks at him.

"There is a free one? Now free?" she stammers.

"Yes," he repeats, gathers a key, and gestures towards her to follow him.

The bungalow is round, with a view to the tree house, to the rice fields.

"How can it be free?"

"Someone just left, half an hour ago. Wanted to leave tomorrow, but changed plans."

That's why, June realizes. That's why I didn't go to the ruins, but stayed at the rice field. That's why I walked through the gate. Now it all fell into place.

All but one thing, she considers later, after she paid the rate for the bungalow, after she walked back to Raju guesthouse and tried to get back the rate she paid there. Of course, they won't pay back. It's afternoon already. And she paid for the night. So she has two rooms now, while others have none. It's wrong, she concludes, as she moves past huts and fields. In her mind, a scene is forming: her standing there one day, without a room. It will happen, she is almost sure of it now. Two rooms here today, no room somewhere in the future.

Then a thought crosses her mind. Jan. She could pass the room to him, for free, for one night, private shower and real bed. All she has to do is to find him. Or rather: find a place to sit along the strip, and wait for him to walk by. Maybe the shop she saw in the morning, with the small restaurant attached. There she could have something to eat, too.

A mere ten minutes later, she sits on a red plastic chair next to the small hut. The plastic chair, it's the same like in the Coconut Huts in Benaulim. Hard to believe she was there yesterday, that she arrived here just this morning.

When the waiter finally shows up, June orders a ginger lemon tea, for the memory. "And a bottle of water," she adds. I need to drink more, she tells herself. And I need to write some lines in the diary.

There, on the page, the day hasn't even started, it is white and unmarked yet. June takes her pencil, and sketches the temple, the river, the nutshell boat. Her Shanti hut. Now for a line about the day. She closes her eyes, to search her memory. There it is. Something Halille has said. Or was it Nel?

You start from scratch every time you arrive.

And true it was. Every arrival brought a new home, new ways. New people. The only constant was herself. And not even that. For so far, her mood has been changing on a daily basis. Or maybe she was still arriving altogether, and had gone too fast since the plane landed, there, in Mumbai, just some pages ago.

Sifting through her diary, June is suddenly sure: she should have stayed in Benaulim. Why didn't she change her bus tickets? Or, if they wouldn't change the ticket, simply buy a new one? 170 Rupees, it was nothing. It was a can of coke, a plate of pasta back home. A ridiculous reason to stick to.

Then she remembers the hut. If she would have arrived a day or two later, she might well have been stranded without even one room. While now, she was stranded with two. A fact that brings her back to the initial cause of sitting here. Which was: to find Jan.

Yet, life has it different. Or: chance has it different. For it's not Jan she finds, but someone else. And the encounter doesn't happen there, in the restaurant, but hours later, just a few steps from her hut, and only because she felt like some soothing sweetness to chew on, at the end of this strange day.

"Chocolate bars," she says to the waiter as he passes the tree house.

"At the stall," the waiter answers.

So June gets up, and walks there, to the little stall next to the reception, where some travellers are standing now. One of them catches her attention, as he almost looks like Jose, having dark hair and wearing an orange vest. Even his features are the same. June ponders, and turns around, to get a last glimpse of this someone who could be Jose's twin brother. It's exactly in this moment that the guy in the orange vest turns his head, too, as if he sensed that someone is gazing at him.

And sure as the street vendors in the Colaba Causeway, as the palm trees along Chowpatty Beach, it's him.

"Hello, my friend," he says, as if it would be the normal thing to meet like that.

"Jose!" June still can't believe it.

Now he starts grinning.

"What are you doing here; I thought your plan was going to the North, no?"

"The plan was to have no plan," he reminds her.

"When did you arrive?"

"Half an hour ago. I arrived with a cattle truck from Bijapur."

"You came with a truck?"

The question draws another smile to his face.

"And you are staying here?"

For the first time, a shadow falls on his face.

"No rooms left," he says.

Now its her turn to smile.

"Not here," she tells him.

"Nowhere," he says.

"Unless you meet a traveller who happened to rent two rooms for one night. "Of course, he doesn't understand what she is saying. So she says it again, in plainer words.

"I think I have a room for you."

"A room for me? You?"

Phone calls are made to confirm, bags are shouldered, and five minutes later June finds herself, walking through the night with Jose, to bring him to Raju's guesthouse.

On the way, she tells the story of her day.

"And to imagine that all day I felt silly about having two rooms, and wondered what the use of this situation could be, if any. I even looked for the guy from breakfast, to tell him he could have a room with a real bed and shower for a night."

Jose laughs.

"Well, I am glad you haven't found him, for I sure do need a shower. And a real bed. Haven't had that for two days."

"But where did you sleep?"

"Outside."

"Outside!?"

"It wasn't that bad. After the truck broke down, and the driver couldn't fix it, we made a little camp for the night."

June looks at him. "Your truck broke down?"

Jose nods.

"You know that there are buses and trains coming to this place?"

"Yes, but I missed the train."

"So you took the truck. And it broke down."

"Right," Jose confirms.

"And then, how did you get here?"

"With another truck that was loaded with goats," he tells her, and sniffs at his shirt again.

Vijayanagar

Grains of sand. Coloured grains of sand. Blue and pink. The Indian woman holds them in her hands, lets them trickle through her fingers. Moving her hands, she paints a pattern on the ground.

A flower, June thinks, her hands cupped around a glass of tea, in concentration. A sand flower. On the street. In front of the door.

The woman looks up. June looks away. She doesn't want... What exactly? To come too close? I wouldn't want to be watched either if I were her, she explains to herself. From the café where she sits, she tries to catch another glimpse.

She had crossed the river in the late morning, to check her e-mails and visit the temple she saw from the bus. To walk the way she came, slowly, instead of rushing past it in the back seat of a rickshaw. Back from the temple, she had looked for a place to sit, and instantly had felt drawn to this café, to the table under a tree. But a couple had taken the table already, and so June had moved on, to look for an alternate spot to sit and have something to drink. Only that the next café didn't look that inviting, the tables white plastic, standing in the pouring sunshine. The other tables were plastic, too, she told herself. It was the atmosphere that had been different.

She had walked on, to the point where the strange pink-horned cows had stood, and had sat in the grass, watching the river, the other side, trying to make out the different guesthouses. After a while, she had walked back to the first café. To find that the couple at the table had been just about to leave when she arrived. Perfect, June had thought, as had sat down in the shade. A few minutes later, the Indian woman had stepped out of the door of the opposite building, and started to paint this sand décor, this flower on the street.

The flower. Now it is almost finished. Just some last grains missing. The Indian woman stands for a moment, to look at her work with folded hands. Then she steps back into the house. Maybe it's a special day, June thinks, maybe she was praying. Then she notices the other flowers, in front of the other houses. Patterns of sand, they will fade away with the wind to return the next day, through the hands of women.

June searches for her camera. She needs to take a picture of that moment, of that morning. The moment she has her camera ready, a girl in a long green skirt appears, a backpack over her shoulder, trekking boots on her feet. The girl walks into the street, past the houses. The flowers, June thinks. How can she not notice the flowers. But the girl isn't looking at the ground in front of her. Her eyes are reading the signs on the other side of the road. The restaurant signs. The guesthouse signs.

"Don't!" June wants to scream. But it's too late. Mechanically, the girl's feet move on, her steps crushing the flower.

And she doesn't even know what she did, June thinks, fighting the urge to run after her, to yell at her, to gather the grains that lie scattered in the sun. It takes a while until she manages to accept what just happened, until she can pick herself up and turn to the brochure she bought in one of the stalls, the one that tells about the past of this region. She opens it, and starts to read the first page, titled *The History of Vijayanagar Kingdom*:

"Within a few years after the arrival of Alla-Udin-Khilji in the kingdom of Yadavagiri in the year 1296, all of Southern India was ravaged by the invaders. Indian culture and religion were endangered by this foreign invasion. At this juncture, people united to protect themselves. It was in this backdrop that Vijayanagar was founded."

Yadagida, she thinks, and feels like she sometimes felt in school, when their teachers made them read texts that seemed written to resist comprehension, that just opened more questions, and referred to unknown facts. With a sigh, she gathers her concentration, and gives the text a second try that once more leaves her with the feeling she had missed the last weeks of homework.

"Vijayanagar," she says in a hushed voice, to at least try the sound of this strange word that probably is just another name for Hampi, at least that's as much of a conclusion as she reached so far. Before she turns the page, she looks up, to see if anyone had heard her. And, to her surprise, sees Jan, on a bike, just about to drive by.

Immediately, she waves, and he comes to a stop, in front of her table.

"Hi there," he says. "I almost didn't see you."

"Hi," she answers. "I looked for you yesterday. I had a room for you. With a shower."

"A room?"

June laughs. "It's a longer tale," she says, and starts to tell it. Somewhere after the second sentences, she stops. "Sorry," she says, "I forgot to invite you to sit down. Want some of the lassi, or some water?"

"I won't say no to that. It's too hot already. And this is supposed to be the cooler season."

"My plan for today was to visit the temples," June says, "But then, I just couldn't make myself walk there in the heat."

Jan points at his bike. "Rent a bike," he tells her. "That's the best way to visit the temples. And convenient. Some of the temples are miles off."

June gazes at the bike, then at the cloudless sky.

"Maybe tomorrow. I am not really feeling like doing much today."

Jan studies her face.

"You aren't developing a cold, are you?"

June shakes her head with vigour. "A cold? No way. I think I am just lacking sleep, with all the moving around in night trains and buses."

"Then make sure that you give yourself a rest, and that you drink enough. Also, eat regularly, even when you don't feel hungry."

June salutes. "Yes, doc."

"I wish I was one already;" Jan says. "But back to your tiredness. The problem is that when your body is out of rhythm, it doesn't give you the right signals any more. You're lacking water, but you don't feel thirsty. You should eat, but you don't feel hungry."

"That's what jetlag does?"

"Exactly. So how about some rice with vegetables? Or *chicken masala*? See, they even have Italian pizza here."

"Maybe I'll try that another day, and stick to the banana pancake for now."

"Sounds like a plan."

They share June's glass of lassi, while they wait for the waiter to take their orders.

Everything takes extra time, here, June thinks. Not that she would mind this now. She could sit here for the next hours, right in this spot.

Still, there is a fact that bothers her.

"Or maybe fact is the wrong word," she explains. "The thing is, if I am too tired from the bus trip to realize that I am thirsty, then how come I happen to walk into the right places at the right time?"

"Good question. Chance, maybe," says Jan.

"Normally I am not the lucky type," June objects, and then tells the story of how the table was first taken.

Jan lets the story sink in before he comes up with a possible explanation.

"Maybe you picked something up," he suggests. "Maybe you saw that the glasses of the couple who was sitting here were empty already."

"I can't even remember if they had glasses standing in front of them or not," June objects.

"That's what I mean: that you saw it without really looking, and that the picture somehow settled in a corner of your brain. And that later, that corner of the brain came to the conclusion that the empty glasses might mean that they are leaving soon, and that the table will be free then. Maybe that was the sudden whim you felt."

June tries to grasp the thought. "Would this mean that - intuition is simply a brain function then?"

Tree House Days

There is a family of birds living in one of the branches that hold the tree house. Blue birds with yellow beaks. The young ones, three, in the nest, are still grey, though. Grey and half blind. Sitting there, waiting to be fed, opening their tiny mouths to the shadow that is her mother or father, to the mouth that delivers pre-chewed food, raising their fragile wings for balance only. One day, they will be tall and blue. One day, they will fly, too.

Somehow the sight comforts and saddens June at the same time. She sits there, a shawl wrapped around her shoulders, on some cushions arranged in a corner of the tree house, and feels just like one of those little birds. At least, like the birds, she isn't alone. The tree house is almost a nest itself, a shaded space up here in this tree that feels like oak, but is called banyan, and that offers enough stability and protection to carry a wooden platform with sitting mats and a low table. Space for eight people, when every place is taken. Now they are four. Her and Sarah, who is nursing an upset stomach. And then there are Tim and Sheryl, who will leave this evening, and decided to have an afternoon of rest and reflection before they pack their things and leave for the North.

"Nepal," Tim says, and a twinkle appears in his eyes. "That's where we are going to. Seeing the Himalayas."

"I will go there, someday, too," Sarah says in a dreamy voice. "Nepal and Nicaragua. One day."

Her stomach growls, a clear sign of protest. Everyone laughs. Sarah cringes. "It's the endless dispute of mind against body."

"But then, Nepal is good for the soul," Sheryl says. "As is India."

It's not so much the sentence itself that startles June, but the way Sheryl pronounced it, as if it was a well-known truth, and not the romantic notion of someone out on a round-the-world trip. I need to muse on that, June thinks, and picks up the diary that lies to her left, next to her bottle of water, next to her pack of handkerchiefs. The words, written on a new page, look like a promise rather than a fact. India is good for your soul. June studies the sentence, its possible meaning, dropping out of the conversation as casual as she stepped into it, or into the tree house.

At least that one gets easier here, June thinks. The stepping in and out of places. A task she always had found difficult, even back in her school days. Especially back in her school days, she corrects herself. She tries to remember what they learned back then about India, there, at their grey desks, in geography class with the green tableau in front. India. Their teacher had showed them pictures once, of the biggest cities of the world, their crowded streets, the slums of Calcutta and Delhi. No one ever told them that the bigger part of India wasn't filled with buildings, but with fields. That there were ruins and rivers. On the world map, India had been a flat brown triangle, somewhere on the right side. Back then, she sometimes had tried to sketch this map, had taken a piece of the oil paper her mother used to wrap up her sandwiches in, and scribbled the outlines of the continents. Then she had checked with the real map. She never got it right, no matter how often she had tried to draw the contours.

And now I am here, June reminds herself. If someone had told me this back then, I would have laughed at the mere idea. But now I am here, in this country that somehow has nothing to do with the one our teacher showed pictures of in school.

The memories of the past still surround June when Jan appears at the top of the ladder, balancing a plate in one hand that carries three cups of tea.

He hands one to Sarah, then sits down next to June, and clinks glasses with her as if it were the happy hour and they were sitting in a café and just got served aperitifs. Then he studies her face again.

"So how is my patient this afternoon?"

"Don't ask," June replies. "I still feel so stupid, to sit here in the heat with a cold."

Jan shakes his head slightly. "There is no reason to feel silly. It's a common thing. Most travellers who arrive here from colder climates develop a cold."

"But it's so – how to say..."

"...inconvenient? Well, that's the nature of disease, I'm afraid."

June scowls. "You are so funny."

"Just realistic," Jan points out. "And after all, you found yourself the perfect spot to be sick, here, with a view to the rice fields. This is far better than being caught by a fever in a cheap guesthouse room next to a noisy street."

June bites her lip. "Sorry, I didn't want to take my frustration out on you."

"No worries." He reaches in his pocket. "Anyway, I brought something to cheer you up. *The Ramayana*," he says, and hands her a well-read yellow pocketbook.

"You will enjoy that one," he says, and breaks into a grin that shows he just waited for the next sentence: "It includes all kind of Yadagida places and people. And even better, it tells you the story of how the places and people are connected. So after you read it, most of the ancient paintings and figures you see around in temples and houses on this trip will make a little more sense."

June takes the book, and opens it, curious for the story it holds. Her eyes fixed on the book, she doesn't see Sheryl watching her with sudden excitement.

"*The Ramayana*! How wonderful!"

Surprised, June looks up. "You know it?"

"Yes, I read parts of it. My favourite story is the one about how Ganges came to the earth."

"Ganges? I thought it was a river?"

"Exactly, the river Ganges. As legend has it, it once flowed across heavens, while the earth was dry. Then, one day, an ascetic who spent his life meditating was granted a wish. He wished for the Ganges to descend to the earth. The wish was granted, but the Gods feared that the earth might not be able to bear the flow. So Shiva was called." Here, Sheryl halted. "You know Shiva?"

"It's a God?"

"Yes. Or to be more exact, he is the third form of God, the one that symbolizes the Destroyer. In paintings, he is the one who has long black hair with a female figure nestled in, and water running from it. Or you can identify him by the trident he holds in his hand."

June shakes her head, and cringes. "Oh dear," she explains." And I wondered why Neptune was shown in paintings, here, too."

"That was Shiva, then," Tim says. "Would be interesting to ask an expert once, whether there is a connection between the symbolism, or whether it is pure chance."

"But go on, telling your story of the Ganges," June begs Sheryl.

"The story, right, that's where we were coming from – Shiva was called," she resumes. "And what he did was to break the force of the descending Ganges by capturing her in his locks. The place where this happened is Mount Kailash, which is in the South of Tibet. From there, the Ganges flows to India, passing Varanasi. When you go to Mount Kailash, you can still see the locks that form the stones."

June blinks. "This mountain really exists?"

"Mount Kailash? Yes. It's a holy mountain, for Hindus as well as for Buddhists. Every year, thousands make a pilgrimage to Kailash, to circle the mountain by foot."

Tim sighs. "We tried to get there, too. It's just a bit complicated with the visa, as it is in Tibet."

June lets the story sink in.

"Wow," she finally says. "I had no clue." Then she looks at her book, and back to Sheryl and then Jan. "You knew all this? And that's all in here?"

Jan smiles. "Not all. The thing you might find is, that the more you learn, the more you realize that you really don't know."

Part 5
Bangalore

All Before Breakfast

From one thousand to six million, from the brown ruins of Vijayanagar to the coloured modern day palaces of MG Road, from countryside to computer city, from Hampi to Bangalore.

June has made the move in one rolling night, 2nd Class Sleeper AC, three tier upper bed, 220 Rupees for a train ride that came with two surprises: she could sleep, and the train arrived on time in Bangalore City Station.

Now I am here, she thinks, as she walks down the stairs that lead from the platform to the exit, together with dozens of other passengers who are cascading down into the city like dressed drops of colour. Pink and green. Gold and silver. Red and yellow. A girl passes June, flowers in her hair, fresh as morning dew. The girl walks straight to the line of rickshaws that is waiting, one three-wheeled vehicle after the other, almost forming a second train. June watches as the girl addresses the third driver in the row. They exchange a few sentences, then the driver helps her store her luggage, and she climbs into the cabin.

Now you, June tells herself, and turns to the next car in line, peeking at the little note in her pocket as she walks, just to make sure she get things right. "Airline Hotel, end of MG Road." It was the place where Tim and Sheryl had stayed. "It won't compare to Shanti, but it is on a side street, with a garden restaurant in front. That's where you want to go," Sheryl had explained.

The reply she gets from the rickshaw driver, a man who is half a head shorter than her, is sobering: "No room there, Madam," he says, and shakes his head.

June had been warned about this line. "It is one of the common scams, an attempt to drag the passenger to one of the expensive hotels, where the driver would be paid a commission. Variations of this scam include 'the area is flooded' and 'the hotel has burned down' or similar stories," Tim had told her. "To all those statements, there is one answer that will get you there nevertheless," he had pointed out.

Let's see if it works, June thinks, and tries the answer: "There is a friend of mine waiting for me."

The line does the trick, and after agreeing on a fare, June pushes her backpack into the backseat, and sits down next to it.

It will take about half an hour to get to the hotel from the train station; that was another helpful fact Sheryl and Tim had shared. Half an hour. About the time it took to get from Hampi Bazaar to the ruins of the royal centre on a bike, a ride through fields that were ruffled by wind, along huge stone boulders, and small temples. Here, it was all buildings and traffic and rush. The perfect contrast.

June watched the passing buildings, trying to guess their purpose. A huge building with a glass entrance – maybe an office building. A heavily decorated edifice, maybe a government building or an embassy. A huge oval construction to the left, easy, a stadium. Another huge building, looking like a cube made of small coloured cubes: an apartment block. A shrill cry, an orange bird.

I could go on like this for another hour, June thinks. Move through this unknown maze of streets and crossings, and drink in all those sights and sounds like they were a never-tasted brand of morning coffee.

When they arrive at the guesthouse, June is in high spirits. Now for a room, for a long shower, for an Indian breakfast. Not toast and jam today, but *semolinas* or *idlis*, or some other of those strange sounding dishes she had seen on menus, but never tried before.

"Just a moment," she says to the rickshaw driver, and ventures off to the reception. This time it's the clerk at the desk who has the wrong answer. "Sorry, no rooms," he says.

June stands there, thinking of a reply that could do the trick. "Another guesthouse?" she asks.

The clerk points to a green building across the street. "There," he says, "but I'm afraid they are full, too."

They are, June finds out after she crosses the street. And now, she wonders, what now? She glances at the guesthouses, at her luggage, then at the driver who hadn't tried to scam her, but had tried to tell her the truth.

Not knowing what else to do, June opens her guidebook and searches for the Bangalore page. When she sees the long list of unknown names, she looks up, and sees the rickshaw driver standing there, waiting for her to give him a chance to address her.

"Madam, if you want, I know a hotel," he says.

This hotel is back at the other side of town, June learns while they drive there. She can see the apartment block again, and the stadium, this time to the right. The embassy. The train station. And finally, only a couple of minutes from the train station, the hotel. Rathaan it is named. The desk manager hands her two keys, so she can have a look at two different rooms. A bellhop guides her way, opens the doors for her. The choice isn't difficult. She takes the second room, the one that is a bit smaller, but is painted white instead of maroon.

"Please take a seat for a few minutes while the room is made ready for you," the desk manager says to her, and gestures towards the sitting area a few steps from the reception.

June sinks into the soft cushions, and just started to study the lobby interior, the panelled desk, the mosaic floor, when a young women in a maroon dress appears, carrying a plate with a cup on it.

"Would you like some tea?" the woman asks.

"Oh, that would be lovely," June answers, taken by surprise. Then she remembers to be careful. "How much would it be?"

The young woman looks towards the reception desk, unsure what to say.

"It's free," the desk manager says in voice that lingers between politeness and amusement. Then he lifts a similar cup that stands in front of him. "Cheers," he says. "Welcome to Bangalore."

"Cheers," June replies, and lifts the cup from the plate.

"Have you been here before?"

June shakes her head. "I just arrived," she says.

"Yes," the desk manager answers, as if it was news. "If you are interested, there is a daily sightseeing tour of the city, starting at two o'clock."

June's look wanders down to the tea cup, then up again. "I don't know," she says. "I didn't have breakfast yet," she adds, as if this would explain her difficulties to find the right lines of conversation.

"Of course," he says, as if this was his mistake. "We will have your room ready in a minute, then you can order breakfast from the room service."

"I didn't mean to complain, it is…"

June runs out of words in mid sentence, and stares helplessly at the lift door, as if the explanation would appear there any moment. In a way, it does: the control pad next to the door turns green. With a swift hum, the lift door slides open, and out steps a maid, holding June's room key in her hands, saving both her and the desk manager from further pre-breakfast talk.

A Secret

There are arches leading to arches, all carved out of teak wood, all arranged in a perfect symmetric pattern. There is a hall filled with pillars, like a crown that holds the ceiling. There are balconies flanked by a carefully arranged garden. There is an inscription on a wooden screen. "Abode of Happiness," it says.

A real Sultan has strolled here once. Princesses, too, June is sure of that. Slowly, she walks up to another arch, and lets her hand glide over the wooden pillar while she passes through the gate and tries to imagine its age. It was in 1791 that the Tipu palace was built.

That was the time of the Third Mysore war, her guide had explained. Back then, India had consisted of several states, and had faced the rise of the British colonial power. One of the states which offered strong resistance to the colonial forces was Mysore, which fought several wars. Sultan Tipu participated in all those Mysore wars.

"In fact Tipu's rule started in the midst of a war against the English and ended in the midst of a war against them," the guide had pointed out. "Also he found himself drawn into conflicts with his neighbours, the Marathas and the Nizam, who joined the colonials in their fight against Mysore, short sighted as they were. In the fourth war, Tipu was killed, and the British power took another step forward. In 1803, they concluded their battle with the Marathas. After that, only Punjab in the North remained independent, but not for long. It fell, too, after the two Sikh wars."

Abode of Happiness. Maybe that's what the place was back then, an island of beauty and peace in a world that has turned upside down. Or maybe Tipu had seen the end coming, and built this place as a memorial of an ending era, June ponders, as she walks out into the gardens, to the flower beds that shine in yellow and orange. A tree is standing there that has probably stood there for ages. June glances to the right and left, but the tiny metal sign that is placed in front of the flowers leaves no doubt, it's forbidden to step on the lawn, just like it's forbidden to pick the flowers. Almost in reflex, she checks her watch. It's a quarter to three. Time to meet up with the guide and the others again.

There are three others: an elderly Indian man, wearing a turban and a long cotton shirt over what seems to be pyjama trousers, and a young couple, dressed in Western clothes. The couple is on a holiday trip, that is as much as June understood as they tried to exchange some friendly phrases in the back of the black cab that is their tour vehicle. The guide is also the driver, and he leads them along the outer palace wall now, back to the parked cab. June tries to keep up with him and the others, but the sidewalk is crowded, interrupted by advertising panels that carry cryptic messages, "MOON DREAMS, KRISHNA PLAZA," the poster in front of her says in blue shades. Next is a printed flower arrangement that states "SERA RUPEE MINI MEALS." Then a coloured sign. "CONTACT RAINBOW." June still ponders on that one while the others have reached the cab, and climbs into their seats, the turbaned man taking the passenger's seat again, while the couple sits down in the back, together with June.

Somehow June had expected a tour bus, filled with other tourists, or rather: with other Western travellers. A group where she would blend in, a guide in front who points out the sights as the bus driver drives the bus. The typical package. She should have known that here, nothing is typical. Or that typical here mostly means: different. Swallowing a sigh, June climbs into the cab. But the woman must have noticed her mood anyway.

"Okay?" she says, and gives June a concerned, friendly smile.

"Okay, thanks," June answers, not knowing what else to say.

The cab pulls out into the road, and they become a part of the street again, a part of the meandering traffic, of this never ending procession of motor bikes, rickshaws, cars, cabs, trucks and bicycles that strives onwards to the next crossing, the next street, the next destination, continually honking and passing. June holds her guidebook in her hands, unopened. She has taken it out of her bag to have a look at the city map, to get some orientation, an idea of where they are coming from, and where they are going to, but the floating crowd outside keeps her under its spell, and like in the morning, she realizes that it in fact it is this part she likes most, the moving, the being in between places, while buildings and people are flashing by, offering small glimpses into private worlds:

> *A tiny balcony filled with flower pots, a small green blooming jungle high above the street. Two Indian women chatting on the sidewalk, one wearing a pink sari, the other dressed in red, seemingly untouched by the heat, by the rush. Just like the flowers above their heads, out of view to them, but in matching colours. A motor bike that carries a whole family, father, mother, and three children, placed in between their parents. A food stall at a corner, consisting of a small table with a huge pile of coconuts. The food seller, a Chinese man dressed all in black, holds a giant knife in his hands, ready to strike, like a figure out of a martial arts movie.*

All those roads, June thinks. All those people. All those different ways of life.

Absorbed by the city, she doesn't turn around even when the driver starts to explain something. Yet, he isn't talking English, he talks in

Hindi, and the stream of words filled with meanings June isn't able to understand just adds to the peculiarity of the drive.

June stays in this mood even when the cab stops and they get out, to see the façade of a long building painted in red colours and decorated with Corinthian columns: the Government Museum. They don't visit it, though, only take pictures of the façade, then they turn around to glance at the building of the other side of the street. It's another palace, framed by palm trees. The guide gives some historic facts, but June only pretends to listen, while her eyes wander to the group of kids playing in a yard. Stones, June realizes. They are tossing stones, playing a child's game of Boccia. Just like she once did.

They move on, to a shop that is named "Traditional Crafts." It's a tourist shop, loaded with gifts to bring home. Paintings, statues, vases, wall carpets. Still June can't help to walk through it, to explore all this with the same amazement she had for the streets.

"You want to have a look at the paintings?" one of the shop assistants asks her.

"Yes, I want to have a look," June says, "but I can't buy," she adds, and smiles.

The shop assistant smiles back, and lifts a painting on a table. It shows a figure June met before already.

"Ganesh," she says. "The God of Good Luck, the Remover of Obstacles."

"Yes," the shop assistant answers, surprised, and places a second painting on the table.

June looks at the figure, a boy with a flute. Probably a God, but she isn't sure.

"It's Krishna," the shop assistant explains. "He is both a great God and a shepherd. He plays an ordinary flute, but even the other Gods can't ignore his music."

"That's a beautiful tale."

"It's real."

"Then it's a beautiful reality," June corrects herself. She reaches for her travel diary, to note down the line, then she notices that the shop assistant still stands there, waiting. "Sorry, but really I can't afford to buy any of these paintings."

"It's fine," the shop assistant says. "I knew you wouldn't buy."

For a moment, neither of them says a word. Then June asks the question that has been on her mind for half the day.

"You know, when I came here, I thought India would be more difficult, with everyone trying to scam you. That at least is the core of the stories some travellers tell, that it's the toughest country you can choose to visit. And now I am here, and it's beautiful. And people are friendly and smile. Like you, when you took the time to explain the painting even though you knew I wouldn't buy. I just don't get it."

"It is because of yourself," he says.

"I don't understand."

"You are smiling, and so I am smiling. India is only reflecting your heart."

"That's the secret of travelling here?"

"That's not even a secret," the shop assistant answers, and bows his head just a bit, to signal that the conversation ends here.

Two Petals

The bathroom has hot water. The television has fifty-two channels. The huge bed has extra blankets. Next to it, there's a table with a vase of flowers, a chair with a cushion, a closet with a mirror. June wanders through her room, walks up to the window, peeks out to the street that is still floating with traffic that is highlighted by the orange rays of the setting sun, by another day turning to night.

I'm lucky, June thinks, to have the room in one of the upper floors. One with a view. Even though others probably wouldn't exactly call the area unfolding beneath the window a view, the four lane street, framed by advertising banners and railways. June lets her head sink against the glass, and gazes down on the sidewalk. The sensation of the cold flat surface against her forehead makes her smile. No glass in Shanti, she remembers. The windows there, they were but openings cut in the walls of the bamboo bungalows. Instead of glass, a thin metal net was strapped inside them, to keep the flies out.

Shanti. Just a few hours away. Just a world away it feels. The last afternoon in Hampi, she had spent it in the Banyan Tree restaurant, an open air place Jose had suggested.

"You haven't been there yet?" he had asked, and so they had walked there, had crossed the river not by nutshells, but by foot, not far from the boat point.

"What if I slip and get soaked?" June had asked, as she had stepped into the water.

"You won't slip," Jose had answered. "And if you get soaked, the sun will dry you again."

Barefoot, he had walked in front of her, and she had followed him, had imagined to step in his footprints underwater. It wasn't the water itself that irritated her, but the fact that it was muddy, that you couldn't see where you where going.

"That's the fun of it," Jose had said, and half an hour later, on the restaurant terrace, they had continued those blind steps by ordering dishes she had never heard of before: *masala mathris* and *spicy pani puri, chicken pakodas* and *onion kachori.*

The memory of plates and bowls filled with fresh and fried snacks, with spicy and sweet sauces, with dips in red and green rouses June's stomach. She picks up the bag of chips on the coffee table. Her meal this evening won't compare to the riverside meal, like the room itself, the day, the place, it will be the counterpart of yesterday, it will be cheese sandwiches instead of chicken pakodas, and chocolate biscuits instead of masala mathris. Instead of sitting on a sun terrace, she will sit on this king size bed, and instead of chatting with Jose, it will be zapping through channels.

Which is just the right thing. The mere thought of getting dressed again, of leaving the quiet of her room lets her sink on the bed, stretch her legs and yawn at the ceiling. No stepping out into those ever moving streets this evening, no searching for a restaurant, no finding her way through unknown grounds. It's enough that she has to pack her things again already, or at least has to decide on what to wear tomorrow, on the bus trip to her next destination, to Mysore. She had planned on taking the train, but that would have meant getting up at five in the morning.

"Why don't you join the bus," the desk manager had suggested. "It will pick you up at nine here at the hotel, and you even get to do some sightseeing on the way."

"Some sightseeing?"

"Yes, you would join a sightseeing bus to Mysore, but instead of returning in the evening, you would stay in Mysore. Lunch is even included that way."

"But it would cost more?"

"It wouldn't cost that much more. The train is about 200 Rupees, the bus trip 500 Rupees, which still isn't really expensive."

It didn't take June long to decide. Arriving on one day and leaving the next day was a rapid pace anyway,

"The other option is to skip Bangalore altogether, and move straight on to Mysore," Sarah had said. "But that would mean twelve hours in the train to Bangalore, and as there are no direct trains, a stop there. And then another couple of hours from there to Mysore. So you can as well split the journey, and spend a day in Bangalore."

"I don't know. One day, it sounds like being gone before you have arrived," June had objected.

Sarah had giggled. "I like this image. It reminds me of a story I once heard, about a group of explorers in Africa. They had arrived at the coast by ship, and then hired Africans to carry their gear. Then they started, walked the first day until late afternoon, set up the camp, and then marched on the next morning. Then, somewhere on the trail, the Africans stopped, and sat down. 'What are you doing?' one of the explorers said. 'Get up and move on.'

The Africans refused. 'Our bodies were moving too fast,' one of them explained, his voice sober and serious. 'Now we have to wait for our spirits to catch up.' And thus, they remained sitting."

The story, there was something about it, but June hadn't been able to draw the conclusion.

"But wouldn't that mean I should rather take two days in Bangalore?"

Sarah shook her head. "It's not so much about the time you spend in places. It's more about the balance between movement and rest. One day can be long, if you use it the right way."

"But Bangalore is huge. Just look at the list of sights that are there to be visited: The ancient Bull Temple, on a hill. Bangalore Palace, that is supposed to look like Windsor Castle. The city market. I love markets! And here: Lalbagh Botanical Garden, a must see, named after all the red roses growing there. There is no way to fit all this into one day without rush."

"Then don't fit it all in. You can't see everything anyway. And there is no need for it, either."

They had paused there, for a moment. Then Sarah had picked up a pen, and opened June's guidebook on the first page.

"May I?" she asked.

"Sure," June had answered, curious for what would happen next.

Sarah had started to write, and in between words, had explained what she was doing. "It's just a quote," she had said, "a little piece of advice once handed to me by another traveller."

She had finished the sentence, and then started to sketch a rose underneath the words. "It was the roses that made me remember it," Sarah added, and finished the flower.

The quote and the flower, it is now a memory that kept travelling with her inside the pages of her guidebook: "You're only here for a short visit," Sarah had written. "So make sure to stop and smell the flowers."

"I did," June answers the line, in thoughts, in words said to herself, and opens the handkerchief that she had carefully placed on the window after the tour. It carries two rose petals, picked from the grounds of Lalbagh Garden, the sightseeing stop they had made after Tipu Palace. They, too, will now accompany her. "And when I am home, I will send one to you. A well travelled petal, carrying an invisible meaning," she whispers, and feels very childish and very wise at the same time, there, in this city, on this bed, in this moment.

Part 6
Mysore

Chamundi Hill

On the right side, there is a huge parking lot filled with red, blue and white buses. At its entrance, a statue of a figure who looks like an Indian pirate with its black beard, its ornamented trousers and its posture, holding a giant dagger raised in the one hand, and a huge striped snake in the other hand.

Beyond the figure, a glimpse of a white temple, and a walkway that is leading there, framed by a string of food stalls. The first one sells postcards and film. The second is loaded with stacks of red and blue bottles. Next to it, a closed red shop with a huge poster on top, advertising yellow ice cream. "WELCOME" is printed on the poster, and "OH WHAT A."

Day, June fills in the missing word, and walks up to the stall that sells bottles and is plastered all over with Enjoy-stickers.

"Yes, Madam," the man behind the counter says to her.

"A bottle of water," June replies, and points at one of the blue bottles.

While he opens the lid of a fridge, and rummages inside for a bottle, June's eyes return to the statue.

"Who is this?" she asks after the man hands her the water.

"Mahishasura," he says, decidedly.

"And what did he do?"

"Mahishasura," the man answers again, laughs, and cuts the air with an imaginary knife.

June doesn't know what to make of this. Get away, she tells herself. Pretend to understand the joke, pretend to think this it's funny, too, then get away. She laughs an artificial, broken laugh, and then abruptly says "Goodbye" and turns. A few steps further, she is part of the crowd again that moves towards the temple, and the laughter of the mad bottle seller is swallowed by the voices around her, by the vibration of foot steps. Surrounded by others, she enters a second row of stalls, their roofs connected by layers of fabric that someone has spun up there, to bring some shade, or to create a feeling of seclusion. The tape played by one of the stalls adds to this atmosphere, some chanting in high pitched voices, or maybe it's the loud speakers that blur the sound.

A few metres further, suddenly live music: a sitar player who sits underneath a twisted tree, in front of a pyramid of neon-coloured postcards that carry the faces of Gods. There is Ganesh surrounded by a red glow, Krishna with blue skin on a golden throne, playing his pipe. There is Shiva, standing in a forest, a lion to his right, a cow to his left. But something is wrong with the picture. June takes a second look, and then she sees it: the figure is two persons. Or rather: a person with a male left side, and a female right side. Half Shiva, half someone else. And there is a monkey dressed in pink, a crown on his head. In his left hand, he carries a golden instrument, in his right hand he balances something that looks like a pyramid. Or a mountain.

"Who is this?" she asks, and looks at the sitar player.

But the player doesn't hear her, he remains in his position, his legs folded, the seven strings of his instrument the single centre of his attention.

June looks at the postcards again, then at him. Maybe they are not his postcards, she thinks. Or maybe she has asked the wrong question. Maybe they are only for those who know, who don't ask ignorant questions.

Slightly frustrated, June walks on, through this maze of mixed impressions. Somewhere, there must be a grill, there is a taste of burned spices is hanging in the air, together with a cloud of sandalwood that seems so dense you can touch it. Incense sticks, June realizes a few metres further. Incense sticks in front of a small stone statue that is standing there, between stalls, caught in the crowd, in the spin of sights and scents just like her.

I need to get out of this, June thinks, feeling a wave of claustrophobia forming in her stomach, I need to get into an open space. She tries to accelerate her steps, but to no avail. The walkway is filled with a thick human stream that floats onwards in one pace, offering no chance of surpassing or overtaking. Okay, June tells herself, and starts counting steps, one two three, one two three. Just let the others carry you along, three two one, three two one. The row of stalls can't go on forever.

It's the counting that makes her remember a phrase she had heard, a few days ago: Put your mind to zero. Three two one zero. Three two one zero, she whispers, and with the third zero, the plastic ceiling comes to an end, and the sky above becomes visible again. Some last stalls, like gates, then a huge free space. The stream of people spills into it like a river into a lake, losing direction and momentum, coming to a halt.

On the other end of the plaza, the temple. White and tall, decorated heavily with figures and ornaments. Seven stories high, each level guarded by two statues with four hands. On its top, a figure in a throne, so high that June can't even make out the face. The colourlessness of the building is what strikes June most. No pink, no red, no blue. No music dazzling from it. Nothing but those ethereal figures that live beyond visibility.

And a clock. A profane clock in between the two figures of the first level. It tells the time in black and white: ten minutes to two. About half an hour until the bus leaves. June looks around, looks for a place to sit, a place of comfort and quiet. There are some benches close to the temple, but of course, they are all taken. There is a small wooden podium, where groups of people step up and down. Maybe a ritual, June thinks, and watches the next group enter the podium, six women, all dressed in blue and white. They stand in a line, while a man opposite them raises – a camera.

June chuckles. Yes, a ritual. Only that it isn't historic, or religious.

Animated by the sight, she draws her camera, too, and takes a picture of the temple. And maybe a picture of the plaza, she thinks, and walks up to the stone wall that surrounds the temple area. While she focuses the camera on different groups of people – an Indian family here, a Japanese bus group there – she notices a second walkway, leading along the outer temple wall. No stalls there, no music. Not many people either. Instead, a view across the land below: forests and fields. White spots: houses. Tiny lines: roads. A gathering of white: the city. A world in miniature. Or simply: the world seen from a distance.

At a bench, she stops for a rest, and looks out over Mysore. Soon I will be there, she thinks. Soon I will walk those streets myself. And then I will move to Cochin. And meet Nel and Faye there.

She hadn't expected to hear from them. Sure, they had talked about meeting up again at the ocean, had even tossed options, Varkala maybe, this cliff beach in the South. Or Cochin, this city with a Portuguese touch. But they also had talked about extended backpack trips and alternate lifestyles, of finding the perfect beach and of conditions for world peace, there, in the coconut huts, and thus, the idea of meeting up again had sounded more like a wish that was unlikely to turn to reality.

Even when Faye's name popped up in her e-mail box, she hadn't connected that to their hazy plan of getting together again. But there they had been, those lines that said:

```
We are here in Fort Kochi,
staying in a small lovely
guesthouse, if you want,
we'll make a room reservation
for you, just let us know.

Looking forward to seeing
you.

Love & Light
Faye & Nel
```

She had written back, there, in the internet café, under a spinning wooden fan. She checked the calendar, to not mess up dates.

```
I'm on the way. Make a
reservation for me, arriving
Thursday the 11th. Can't
believe this works out!
```

That had been yesterday, in Bangalore. And now, Mysore. And at this time in two days, it would already be Cochin, and Faye, and Nel.

It's unreal, June thinks, as she slowly moves on, toward the end of the walkway. It's simply unreal, she repeats, when she reaches the pirate again, standing there, frozen in time, just like the snake in his hands.

Beyond the pirate, there is a flat building she hasn't noticed when she arrived. Its entry is framed by two signs: "GODLY MUSEUM" and

"ENTRANCE FREE" they state. A young woman in a pink dress is just walking out of it. Drawn by curiosity, June walks in, to find herself in a room that has more the feeling of a class room than a museum: the only objects inside are painted panels hanging on the walls, showing scenes of the troubles of worldly life, and of the blessings that come through spirituality. One of the panels holds the vision of a perfect, unified world. Another panel carries an inscription:

> *5000 years ago at this time*
> *you have visited the same place*
> *in the same way you are visiting now*
>
> *World drama repeats itself*
> *all 5000 years.*

June reads the inscription again, then copies it into her diary, while she lets the concept of world drama cycles sink in. When she walks out, she can't help but see herself, walking out of this place 5000 years ago, with the same unanswered questions in mind. Maybe that's why I am here again, she thinks, and feels tempted to leave a message for herself somewhere, in this place. But what kind of message would remain through all those centuries?

Alice without a Manual

"Masala Dosa," Carla says. "You have to try the Masala Dosa next time."

June laughs. "I already had my share of it today ," she explains. "In an Indian road stop café. That was fun."

"An Indian road stop café?" Carla asks.

"I took a sightseeing bus from Bangalore to come here. And they had this break, halfway to Mysore, out in the middle of nowhere. And all there was to order was Masala Dosa, as they didn't expect foreigners on the tour."

"So you had that," Carla says.

"Yes. Together with the unexpected glory of being the main attraction for fifteen minutes, as everyone looked at me to see how the foreigner would cope with the fact that in this place, the food was served without cutlery."

Carla picks a knife and a fork out of a plastic cup that stands in the middle of the table, and lays them out in front of June. "Well, then welcome back in the exquisite world of eating with tools."

They had met the same way June had met Kim, back in Mumbai. Only that this time, the roles were the other way round: it had been June who found a place already, and Carla who stood there between tables, unsure where to turn.

"If you want to, just take a seat here," June had offered, forwarding the favour.

"Thanks," Carla had answered, and taken the chair opposite June. "I didn't expect it to be so full." Then she had stared at her watch. "It's half past seven already," she had said, in disbelief. "What a day. I have been visiting the palace this afternoon, and somehow lost track of time."

A few minutes later, just after Carla had ordered, Pascal had walked through the terrace door and joined their table after he had seen Carla. So suddenly, instead of a solo dinner, June now is part of a vivid conversation.

"The palace. How is that?" June asks, returning to the topic.

Carla opens her arms, to express the size. "Huge. There is one entrance, not far from here, but it's closed. I thought I could walk to the other entrance, but you really have to take a rickshaw to get there."

"And how is the inside?"

"It is…" Carla starts to say, but then stops in mid sentence, at a loss for an appropriate description.

"Over the top," Pascal finishes the statement. He picks up the straw hat he had placed on the table when he arrived, and turns it upside down, as if words weren't enough in this case. Then he reverses the move. "Or, on a more neutral note, call it fascinating."

"But it's worth visiting?"

"Definitely. It's probably the most interesting sight Mysore has to offer. Try to arrive there around noon, then all the tour groups are on lunch break, and it's not so crowded," Pascal suggests.

"I haven't thought of it, but that makes sense. Thanks for the advice."

"You're welcome. And when you are there, join one of the guided tours. They have them in different languages, and the background information is essential to make sense of the whole place. Otherwise you might feel like Alice wandering through Wonderland without a manual."

June sniggers. "That's exactly how I felt today. Right there, in Wonderland, or rather: on Wonderhill, without a manual."

"You've been to Chamundi Hill already? I thought you just arrived?" Carla asks, surprised.

"That was part of the bus sightseeing tour that brought me here. Only that there was no guide included, and so I still have no clue what the hill and the pirate statue up there was all about."

Pascal looks at her, puzzled. "Pirate statue?"

"Yes, the big statue in front of the walkway that leads to the temple. With the guy that holds a snake in his hands."

"It's a tale, I think I read about it in the guidebook …" Pascal says, and starts to dig through his bag, "…but I think I haven the guidebook with me. Too bad."

"The guidebook," June says, and her eyes spark as if someone just handed her a key. "I am so silly. I left mine in the bus, as it is so heavy to carry around, and then later didn't even consider checking it."

"I know what you mean," Carla says, and produces a pile of paper that is held together by a rubber band. "I cut mine in pieces. Here is Mysore," she says, and starts to flip through the pages. "And here is the description of Chamundi Hill. Now let's see," she says, and hands the page to June.

"That's from the same book I have," June says, surprised, and starts to read:

"Mysore was once the capital of the old Royal province of Mysore. As legend has it, the people of Mysore used to be troubled by the demon Mahishasaru. One day, the Goddess Chamundeshwari appeared on a hill near Mysore, and fought the demon. Since that time, the royal family has worshipped Chamundeshwari as the palace deity. The hill where the fight took place was named Chamundi Hill. On top of the hill, a temple dedicated to the Goddess was built, as a symbol for victory of good over evil. Later, a statue of the demon Mahishasaru was added."

Ending the sentence, she lets the page sink.

When she looks up, her eyes meet Pascal's, and for a second they just sit there, looking straight in the iris of the other, into this coloured sphere that creates images in one's mind. Green, she thinks. He has green eyes.

"Your..." he starts to say. Then his voice trails off, and he starts to cough.

"Your pirate. So it is a demon," he finally manages to say.

It wasn't the initial sentence, June can feel it. Or was it? She looks at Carla, who seems unconcerned, and still contemplating on the history of Mysore.

"When I remember it correctly," Carla says, when she sees June's inquiring look, "the demon's name – what was it again? – is now part of the city's name."

Maybe it's all been in my mind, June tells herself, and lifts the page again, to glance over the next paragraphs. It doesn't take long to find the explanation.

"You are right," June replies. "The word Mysore is a short form of 'Mahishasurana Oore' which means: The Town of Mahishasura."

"There you are," Carla says.

June shakes her head, once for the imagined look, twice for her own silliness. "And to think that I had the answer in my bag all the time. And wasn't even aware of it."

She picks up the page as if it was a precious document, and hands it back to Carla, who sorts it in her pile of ripped guidebook pages, while a smile plays around her lips.

"Thinking of it, isn't that what they always say about answers: That you walk the whole world in search of them, just to find that they waited back home, on your doorstep?"

Almost in reflex to the words, June's eyes focus on the terrace door, as if the answer really would materialize there, if only she concentrated hard enough on it.

Instead, the waiter appears, balancing plates in his hands.

"Our dinner," June says, and it's only then that she realizes that the others, just like her, have their eyes fixed on the doorway.

"So that is the answer for the day, then," Pascal mocks, while he studies the dishes.

"Chicken Tikka and Stuffed Parathas."

Again, June can't escape the feeling that he intended to say something else. Without planning it, she replies in a twisted line, too.

"Yes, that's the answer," she says, keeping the tone of her voice serious. "And like always, it induces another question: will the answer be too spicy for us to enjoy it?"

Double Headed

Three white doves are crossing the eight triangles of ornaments that form the mosaic dome of the palace pavilion. The pattern of the mosaic is mirrored in the floor. From two sides, hallways lead to stairways that lead to other hallways, to rooms filled with caskets, with mementos, with glass paintings of glorious processions of the past. The doors, made of thick, dark wood, are carved and decorated with shields of power.

"Please look at the stained glass that covers the ceiling," the guide says. "Their peacock motifs symbolize grace, pride and beauty. Exactly what you would expect in the 'Kalvana Mantapa,' the marriage pavilion."

He turns to his group for a moment, like a teacher checking on his pupils. Then he points at the ceiling again. "See the magnificent chandeliers. They are coming from Czechoslovakia. The tall, beautiful iron pillars that are arranged in groups of three at the corners of the central octagon – they were brought from Scotland, while the shining tiles of the floor were imported from England."

The guide keeps on talking and pointing, yet instead of following his explanations, June's eyes follow the flight of the three white doves, up there in the artificial sky that is formed by glass and metal. The pavilion must feel like a huge bird cage to them. Or like a personal palace, with visitors who cross their floors during daytime, who stand there, moving their heads in all directions, up, down, to the left, to the right, dazzled by the multitude of colours and patterns, dazed by the glorious memories of an era that now is but a memory, a tale of wars lost and won, a nesting place for birds.

Once upon a time, June thinks. Once upon a time, there were princes and maharajas living here; there were royal weddings celebrated in this pavilion. There were magicians walking these floors, reading the fate in the stars. Maybe they had seen it coming, the change of skies, the turn of powers. Maybe they turned into birds, back then, so that they could stay, could keep living here, free from diplomatic matters, from worldly concerns.

As if to remind her that she is still standing on the other side of this fantasy, down on the trouble-ridden grounds of the world, the guide signals that its time to move on, to the next room. June is tempted to drop off, to simply remain in the shadow of one of those pillars. But the guide looks straight at her, as if he could read her thoughts, and so she skips the idea and turns towards the exit instead, to follow the others who are already walking through the hallway that leads to the next floor.

Upstairs, the guide leads them through another hallway that is framed with ancient paintings. "They are just the aperitif, so to say," the guide explains. "The real masterpieces wait beyond this corridor." In a dramatic gesture, he opens the curtains at the end of the floor, and leads them into a gallery – an extravagant hall filled with ornamented pillars, oil paintings and marble statues. June doesn't know where to look first, and so her eyes, in search of a break of all the artistry, wander to the balcony that offers a view to the gardens below, to a square of yellow roses next to a water fountain. That's where she had rested for a few minutes after she arrived, on those stone steps in the shade. Now there was someone else sitting there, a guy with a straw hat.

Pascal, she thinks.

"One of the famous traditional gold-leaf paintings," the guide states.

He knew I would be here, and so he came to meet me.

"And here, a portrait of the twenty-fourth Wodeyar Raja, who rebuilt the palace in 1912 after it got burnt down in 1897."

June takes a quick look at the portrait, then turns to the figure in the garden again. It is him. She is almost sure of that, even though she can't see his face, and even though he probably isn't the only one wearing a straw hat in this city.

"Let's turn to the next painting," the guide orders. "Here you see, a double headed eagle. This is the Mysore royal symbol."

What now. She can't simply walk away from the group, can she? And what shall she say when they meet?

Hello, for a start, an ironic voice murmurs inside her head. That is, if it's him at all. Otherwise, you just walk on towards the exit, and return to reason while you are at it.

It's him, she argues, and takes another step toward the balcony, willing the figure in the garden to move, to show his face, just for a moment.

Yet the figure remains idle.

See, the inner voice states, if it was him, he would turn now. That's at least how it happens in all the romantic movies.

But this is the palace of Mysore, not a part of a movie, June argues in a hopeless effort to fight irrationality with its own weapons.

Breathing Lessons

"So you learn those things like to stand on your head, or to bend yourself into weird positions?"

"Yes and no," Pascal says. "The idea of yoga isn't to make you able to compete with circus artists. The postures, they are meant to help you find balance for the mind and the body."

"Balance? But they look so edgy," June says, and entangles her hands the way she did when she was a kid. To her surprise, her hands still know the position.

"Like this, see," June says, and wiggles with one of the fingers. "Now can you tell which finger this is?"

She watches as he gazes at her hands. Of course he can't tell. Yet, instead of asking her to unfold her hands, to show him how she did this, he touches the finger in question with the tip of his index finger. Then he looks at her, and there it is again. This moment of eyes looking into eyes. Like the day before. Only that this time, it's she who breaks the spell, who lowers her eyelids and scatters some words, to return to safe ground.

"Can you..." she says and taps his index finger in return, as if the look had been nothing but part of this child's game, "...can you do this, too?"

"I am afraid we haven't learned that one in classes, yet," he says. "But if you want, I can show you one of our teacher's favourite exercises."

"Right here?" June says.

"Right here," Pascal answers. "Feel free to collect the coins, in case someone offers a donation."

"You aren't serious, are you?"

"Now I am," he says, in a quiet voice, and draws his feet towards him. In one swift move, he crosses his legs, straightens his back, sets his hands on his knees, and closes his eyes, transforming from a guest in a coffee shop who just sipped his tea, to a timeless human Buddha sculpture who happens to sit there, in this small café in a side street, a few minutes from the palace, far from the pompous glory of oil paintings and carved pillars, at this low wooden table, surrounded by simple cushions instead of chairs.

June turns her head, to see if some of the other guests are following the scene, but no one seems to be paying attention. What next, she wonders, and studies Pascal's face, his composed features, waiting for the next move, for the exercise he spoke of. Yet, instead of turning to another posture, he remains idle for a minute, then for another.

Finally his eyes open again. "Now, how was that?"

"I thought it would be somewhat … more moving," she says, still unsure if he is serious or not. In all respects, that is. Yes, he had waited in the palace garden. But when she had asked if he came there for her, he hadn't answered, had simply moved to another topic. And yes, they were here now, having a tea together. And talking about postures, of all topics. Postures.

"You think I am kidding you?" Pascal asks, obviously noticing her doubts.

"Are you?" June replies with a question.

He shakes his head. "I am not playing tricks," he says. "It really is the favourite exercise of our teacher. And it is the most graceful of yoga postures, too: the lotus. Inducing the perfect balance between activity and rest. It helps to quiet the mind, to leave the constant stream of thoughts that follows you all day."

"And what where you thinking when you were sitting there?"

"The point is not to think something. All you do is to focus on your breathing."

"And it works?"

"Yes," he says, then grimaces. "And when it doesn't, it at least makes for interesting struggles with your own thoughts."

June looks at Pascal, then at the others. No one seems to mind their moves. "Let me try this," she says, and draws her feet towards her. When they form a triangle, she rests her hands on her knees, and looks at Pascal. "Like this?"

"That looks good already. Just try to sit a bit more straight," he says, and demonstrates the posture for her again. "Imagine someone has placed a bowl on your head."

"Okay," June says. "And now?"

"Now, close your eyes, and imagine that your thoughts are resting in this bowl, while you are breathing in... and out. In... and out. In... and out..."

At first, all June concentrates on is Pascal's voice. It's only after the second out that she remembers to focus on her breathing. To her surprise, it is already in tune with his words. In... and out. In... and out. The voice, and her breath, they unite to a sensation of peacefulness that seems to be moving through her, like air, like sound. In... and out.

I don't want this to end, June suddenly thinks. Please, don't let this end.

"And when a thought arises, then let it be, and just return to your breathing," Pascal says, as if he could hear her think.

"I'll try," June whispers, then bites her lips.

"Shhh..." Pascal says.

June tries to relax again, to concentrate on his voice.

"In... and out..." he resumes. "In... and out..."

But the damage is done. The quiet of mind, it doesn't want to return to her.

Part 7
Cochin

Everything is Easy Once

"A ticket for the ferry," June says.

The tiny old man places the cigarette in the ashtray next to him. "Fort Cochin?"

"Yes, Fort Cochin."

"Twenty Rupees, Madam."

June digs in her pocket, and produces two coins. She places them on the counter, together with a question: "When will the ferry be here?"

"Just coming," the tiny old man says.

Just coming. That could mean anything from five minutes to half an hour. It's fine with June.

"Is there still time for a cup of chai?" she asks.

"Yes, yes," the tiny old man answers. "Always enough time for a chai," he says, and hands her the ticket, a thin slice of green paper, with a number on it. Then he shuffles away, and shouts something into the semi-darkness of his cabin.

"Chai coming, Madam," he says to June, as he returns to the counter, and picks up his cigarette again.

"Thank you, Sir," June replies, and slides the ticket in the front pocket of her waist bag, so that she will have it at hand when she boards the ferry. Then she looks for a place to sit. There are no benches, no chairs. Just a dock for the ferry, and the hut of the ticket seller. Behind it, a dusty car park. And to the right, some stacks of dried wood. Almost a bench, June thinks, and looks for a comfortable spot to sit, one with a view to the water.

Just when she settled, a young boy appears, with her cup of tea. June picks another coin out of her pocket, to pay for the tea. This is perfect, she thinks, as she folds her hands around the hot cup, and takes the first sip of the sweet chai, there, at the waterfront, with a view to a huge freighter coming in, and a small fisher boat going out.

Watching the boats move through the water, she recounts the path of her own journey in her mind. The plane from Milano to Mumbai. The arrival there, and her first ride in an Indian taxi. Through the darkness, to the centre of Mumbai. Then the night train to Margao. The taxi to the beach of Benaulim. The rickshaw to the Metropolitan in Margao. The ride in the night bus to Hampi. The rickshaw ride to the train station in Hospet, in the fading light of the day. The night train to Bangalore. The extended taxi ride through Bangalore, in the early morning, in search of a place to stay. The sightseeing bus trip to Mysore, with a stop on Chamundi Hill. The rickshaw to Hotel Tiffany's, the place where she stayed in Mysore. The rickshaw from there to the train station of Mysore. The night train to Cochin.

And then, Cochin central station. As always, flocks of rickshaws waiting, together with another ride through an unknown city. Cochin in the morning. Small streets and wonderful old houses in pastel colours. Wild flowers at a street corner, orange and yellow. A market to the right, a block of buildings to the left. The waterfront. The ferry station. And now to come, the crossing to Fort Cochin.

June had always worried most about those parts, about the passages from one place to another. How to manage those steps, how to find the way to the right train, to the right bus, she had wondered. As it had turned out, the answer was easy. Just tell the rickshaw driver where you need to go, and he will take you there. And to be on the safe side, ask someone from the guesthouse what the running rates are. Or, if you forget that, then ask another passenger before you get off the train. Easy as that. But then, everything is easy, once you have learned how it works.

Just like dealing with the time spent in buses and trains. Back home, when she planned the trip, and read about those eight hour bus rides

and twelve hour train journeys, she had felt drained just by the thought
of being stuck for hours in a sticky, bumpy bus or train compartment.
And the idea had even seemed worse after she had arrived in Mumbai,
and had felt tired just by the thought of organizing a way to get to the
other side of the city and back. "How did you cope with all those endless
rides?" was one of the first things she had asked Kim, there, at the table
in Leopold, during June's first Indian lunch with another traveller.

"It's exhausting," Kim had explained, "but at the same time it's
energizing. To see all those houses and fields, to ride all those roads, to
be moving endlessly through these nets of small villages and huge cities.
I mean, that's what travelling is about: to be on the road. To really feel
the asphalt. To carry the dust of the places you passed in your clothes.
That's the way to do it."

And it was. Tiring and reviving at the same time. Just like Kim had said
it would be. I have to write her, June thinks. Tell her that I am here, in
Cochin. Not in an e-mail, but in real ink, written on the back of a picture
that is printed on paper, and that will travel halfway round the world
before it reaches her. That will go with a boat, with a truck, with a plane.
And then, probably, with a train, and a truck, and a car. Until it reaches a
blue letterbox somewhere in Canada. At least that is how June images
Kim's letterbox to look like: painted blue, standing in front of a small
wooden house.

Dreamer, June tells herself, and watches another ship get closer. Maybe
the ferry that will carry her to Faye and Nel. Who are staying in one of
the popular guesthouses, where a room is waiting for her. A sun beam
plays on June's face as she foresees the conversation with the rickshaw
driver at the island jetty in her mind:

"Sorry, Madam, but the Elite is full," he will say.

"There are friends of mine waiting there for me," she will answer. And
this time, it won't be a trick to ward off a scam, as it was in Bangalore.
Here, in Cochin, it will be the truth.

Circles in the Sand

There are nets laid out in the sand. Young men in Nike t-shirts and in baggy trousers crouch over them, fixing holes by knotting yet another string into them. A few metres further, boats rest in the sun. They probably had been out in the early morning, bringing in fish that is now set up in lines in the stalls of markets, waiting for buyers.

Beyond the boats, there is a bamboo platform, erected in the water, holding a wooden structure that looks like a giant swing. Stones on the one side, up in the air; a net on the other side, low in the water.

A fisherman, dressed in red and black, leans on the centre pole, almost as if he was part of the structure. And he is, in a way. For it takes his swift moves, a rearranging of weights, a pulling on a string, to set the stone swing in motion, to raise the net from the water. With a splash, the fish land on the bamboo platform. Silver, they glitter in the sun. The fisherman collects them carefully, and then cuts their heads off with a knife he carries in the waistband of his trousers.

"They are called Chinese fishing nets," Nel explains. "Traders from China introduced them here. That was in the days the Kublai Khan was ruling, when Mongolia was a huge empire."

June picks up a hand full of sand, and lets it rinse through her fingers, forming a small pyramid under her hands. Just when the last grains of sand fall from her hands, a huge freighter comes in sight, and passes behind the knotted nets, behind the sand pyramid, scattering the illusion of being somewhere far from civilization.

June cringes, but Faye gets her camera out, and takes a picture. "That's the great thing about this place," she says. "It is like an island that is swinging between centuries. And between cultures."

She gestures towards a pink building beyond the strip of fishing nets. "See this house? It was built by the Portuguese. They also were the ones who brought Catholicism to this place. And with it, their architecture, and culture. Back then, Goa was the capital of the Portuguese eastern empire, that was stretching from East Africa and Arabia to Japan."

Amazed, June stares at the house, waiting for a historic figure to appear on one of the balconies of the upper stories. But the wooden doors remain closed.

"And now guess the name of the square that is now populated by fish stalls," Nel says.

"I have no clue. Portuguese Square?"

"Almost. It's Vasco da Gama Square."

June shakes her head slowly, as if slight movements would help to grasp surreal facts. Still, there is one thing that doesn't seem to fit. "But how did they come here?"

Instead of answering, Faye points at the ships. "All by boat."

"Right," June says, and suddenly all falls in place. "That's why they landed on the coast."

Another boat is passing, a smaller one, with a green sail. "ODYSSEUS 2" is written on its side, in turquoise letters.

"Odysseus," Faye says. "Those were the real days of travelling. When you went without a guidebook, a credit card, or a return date. When you had no clue about the places that were waiting for you, there, on the other side of the ocean."

"Those were the days, my dear..." Nel declares, and picks up a hand of sand, to let it rinse through her fingers, like June. Yet instead of reaching the ground, the grains of sand are carried away in a breeze, and fade in a dusty haze.

"...And these are the winds that carry you away from here," Faye concludes Nel's words.

"Oh, please," June moans, "Don't talk about leaving already, when a part of me hasn't even arrived here." She gazes out to the water, as if there was a boat out there, beyond the horizon, that was on the way to deliver the rest of her.

"Are you sad?" Faye says, picking up her mood even before June named it.

"No," June answers, and picks up a stick, to paint patterns in the sand. "Or yes," she suddenly says, "but maybe melancholic would be the better word. Or: stupid."

She looks at Faye, then at Nel, and then starts to tell her tale, this tale of Chamundi Hill, of meeting Carla, of looking into Pascal's eyes, and of meeting him again in the garden of Mysore palace.

"When I think of it now, the whole day was like out of a movie," she says. "Even the hotel I staid in, Tiffany's. I chose it by name. I saw it in the guidebook, and I just knew I had to stay there, so that I could feel like Audrey Hepburn in the morning, and have a real breakfast at Tiffany's."

"And you had it?"

"Well, I had the Bollywood version of it. They don't have a breakfast hall, instead they have room service, and so I called and asked what they would recommend for breakfast beyond tea and toast. Idlis and Sweet Semolina was their suggestion. How does this taste like, I asked. Ah, just like Idlis and Sweet Semolinas taste like, was their enlightening answer.

"But then, how to explain things like that, I thought, and so I tried it. And it was perfect. Served on palm leaves. With the spicy sauces you get with Masala Dosa. Really, I should have taken a picture of this plate, sitting there on my bed, with a view of the peak of a mosque and a dusty palm tree."

"So that was the start of the day."

"Yes. And it went on like that. I looked for a rickshaw, but instead a donkey cart appeared, and so I went to the palace feeling like a gypsy princess. In the palace, I found it hard to concentrate on the guide's explanations, and started to make up tales of the past. Then I saw Pascal. Or rather: his straw hat. And just knew it was him, who came to see me."

"And he waited for you in the rose garden," Faye adds.

"Yes," June says. "It's completely cheesy, isn't it. And then we went to the coffee shop, and talked about travelling, yoga, art, religion, the world, the universe and all. All except us. But when we said goodbye, he took me in his arms, and held me."

Nel whistles through her teeth. "Sweet," she says. "And then?"

"An then he went to his evening class, and I went to Tiffany's, to get my backpack, and leave with the night train."

"And he didn't ask you to stay for another day?"

June shakes her head. "He knew that there was a room booked for me here in Mysore, that you were waiting for me. And then, I had the train ticket already."

"The ticket," Faye says. "Now why does this remind me of Benaulim somehow?"

"Yes, I know," June answers, and cringes. "But then, it was good that I went to Hampi like I planned, because that's how I got a hut in the Shanti Lodge, and how I met Jose again, just when he had no room to stay, while I had two."

"I remember the e-mail you sent that day, about the ruins, and those archaic nutshells to cross the river," Fays says, and smiles. "I'm glad they invented the modern type of boats here already," she adds, and gestures toward a ferry that is passing by, loaded with people, motor bikes and bags filled with coconuts. They watch the ferry pass, and move towards another island, further from the mainland.

It's Nel who breaks the silence again, with a thought that had been also been crossing June's mind in the night before.

"Why didn't you ask Pascal to come with you to Cochin?"

"I don't know. I somehow didn't think of it until I was on the train, and then it was too late," she explains.

"You could still ask him," Nel points out the obvious. "All it would take is an e-mail."

June picks up a stick and draws two circles in the sand. With a slow move, she crosses one out. "What if he says no?"

"And what if he waits for a message from you while you sit here contemplating the hypothetical consequences of yet unwritten mails?" Nel answers, takes the stick from June, and, with one swift brush, erases the crossed circles completely, and lays down the stick.

"You think he would come here?"

"Unfortunately, no one ever taught me to tell the future," Nel says.

"Which maybe is the better way to live, anyway," Faye remarks, picks up the stick, and paints a TV in five lines: a box with an antenna sticking it. "Otherwise your whole life would feel like a replay of an old movie. With the endings set before the beginnings even happened."

June sighs, and takes the stick from Faye. "So I guess, the only way to find out what will happen in the next part of this journey – is to ask the question," she ponders, and draws two new circles, right on the screen of the sand TV.

Karma Coffee

Pink oleander in clay pots. A green wooden bench in front of a white house in a side street. The door wide open.

"That's the place?" June asks.

"Yes, that's it," Nel says, and steps into the house.

Inside, an empty room. Empty but for the paintings that line the wall, some of them tiny, in black and white, drawing the visitor close to their surface. Others, huge and in oil colours so thick that the brushstrokes form elevations of paint.

"Look at this," June says, and points at a painting that is made in shades of one single colour, all in green. She steps closer, and studies the lines, the lingering schemes they form.

"It could be a jungle," June says.

"Or a street seen through stained glass."

June takes a step to the left. "That's odd," she says, and moves back to the right again. "It seems to change with the way you look at it."

Nel walks past the painting, her eyes fixed on the canvas. "Yeah," she says, "it does. Cool. What's it named?"

A small card underneath the painting gives the answer. "Karma 3," June reads, and looks at Nel, who still glances at the painting, an amused smile playing on her lips now.

Karma. June had heard the word before. "It means destiny, or… ? But why is it green, then?"

Nel angles her head. "When you look like this, you can see a figure in the painting, see?" she says, then moves her head the other way, and returns to June's question. "It's not exactly destiny. It's rather…"

"Fate?" June guesses. "Or chance?"

"Maybe rather a complex version of the idea 'What goes around, comes around'. According to the laws of karma, everything you do, and even everything you say or think, has a positive or negative effect on the future."

"Oh," June says, and studies the lines of the painting again. "I thought it would be something more mysterious."

"In a way, it is," Nel says. "The consequence of karma would be that there is no such thing as chance. Everything happens for a reason, caused by something done, said, or thought."

"So – ," June starts the sentence, then looks at Nel, surprised. "So we met for a reason in Benaulim?"

"That's at least what the concept of karma says."

The thought staggers in June's conscious like a shimmering soap bubble that resists to fit in the usual process of consideration.

"Then how..." June starts to piece the next question together, yet gets interrupted by Faye, who arrives from the travel agency, some brochures in her hands.

"Hi! You are still in the gallery," she says, and walks up to them. "I thought you were sitting in the café already, sipping Latte Macchiato."

June looks around. "Latte Macchiato? Here?"

Nel grins. "That's one of the other virtues of this place, apart from inspiring paintings: Italian coffee."

"And cool music," Faye adds, and walks towards a wooden door on the other side of the gallery.

Behind the door, it's Treasure Island. At least that is how it seems to June: An inner courtyard, framed by palm trees and orchids. Tables with benches that are built out of the wall. A Café del Mar mix playing. And in the corner, an espresso machine. Next to it, a shelf that carries yet another surprise.

"Chocolate cake," June whispers, following Faye and Nel to the free corner table that seems to have waited just for them, and for a while, she abandons the reflections on chance meetings, karmic consequences and certain shades of green, and focuses all her attention on the cup and the plate in front of her.

"Obviously that was all I needed," she jokes after she picked up the last crumb of cake, and sipped once more from her Latte. "Not the answer to the great riddles of life, but a massive portion of concentrated sweetness."

Curious, Faye looks from Nel to June. "The answer to the great riddles of life - now when did I miss this one?"

"Oh, that was in the gallery, when you walked right into our conversation, crying for coffee," Nel teases.

"So you were one step away from the solution, and I spoiled it all?"

June sniggers. "Yes, and the effect of your universal disturbance is the instant materialization of chocolate cake, obviously. So no worries. We are right there with you, down on the bottom of Maslow's hierarchy of needs."

"All right. Then where will we move to from here, according to that theory?"

The hierarchy of needs. They once had discussed it in school, and the diagram that had been pinned to the wall in that lesson had showed a coloured pyramid. The physical needs on the bottom, food and water. But what came next? "Wasn't it safety? A place to sleep, shelter from the elements?"

"See, we covered this one already, too," Nel says. "So we can move straight on to the upper levels, and thus, back to the topic we left in the gallery: the question of karma," she ends the sentence, and turns to June.

The question, June thinks. What had been the question that she wanted to ask? In her mind, she moves back to the gallery, the green painting. The changing schemes. All things happen for a reason, Nel had said. They are implied by our own actions that come around as they go around. Or by our thoughts. No coincidences. All just cause and effect. Only it isn't true, June figures. Life isn't fair.

"For if it would work that way, why do some people get away with the crimes they commit, while others are imprisoned even though they are innocent? Or why are some lucky in their lives, and others aren't? And why is it so often those who don't really deserve it are the lucky ones?"

Instead of answering, Nel takes her spoon, and churns the milk bubbles that are drifting on top of her coffee. "Because karma rather works like this," she says, and places her cup in the middle of the table. "It moves in unpredictable ways."

Nel gives the coffee a spin in the other direction, and they all watch how the bubbles gather in the middle, and then float to the sides again. "Also, it moves from one life to the next," she explains. "So the one who gets away with his crime maybe is the one who ends as a beggar in his next life, losing all he had."

June tries to imagine it. A world of infinite justice that moves from one life to the next. Like science fiction. Or rather – she shakes her head, but can't escape the irony of the image.

"It would be like in those video games," she says. "Where you start from the point you reached before you run out of energy. Only that it would be ... like the whole world is connected in the game. And the game never ends."

"Yeah," Nel says. "That's about how it would be. Or how it is."

June stares at the bubbles in the coffee. They are still moving, some alone, some in groups that cling to each other, drawn together by an invisible energy.

"It's a completely different concept of life," she finally states. "It's weird."

"Not so weird," Nel says. "Think of the churches back home, how the people go there and light a candle when they worry about something, or someone, believing that it somehow will make a difference."

"True, you have a point there," June says, and makes another try to grasp the concept. A life that is the reflection of all the things one has done and said. And thought. And yearned for. All the silly dreams and high hopes leaving traces in the present. June chuckles. "Be careful what you wish for, it might come true," she says. "That is karma at work, then?"

"Very much," Nel agrees. "That would be the twisted humour of karma at work."

Thoughtfully, June takes another sip of her coffee. When she places the cup on the table again, she blows on the surface, making the bubbles move again. "And where do go from this viewpoint now?" she asks.

"I don't know," Nel answers, and looks around. "Maybe back to the counter, to order another round of karma coffee?"

Trapped

White birds. A whole flock of white birds. Suddenly they are there, moving through the sky in a huge circle.

June gasps. "Look at them!"

"Seagulls," Nel says. "And they are coming closer."

June gets up slowly, as if any fast movement would disturb the birds' flight. As if they cared about those three humans, who sit there, at the beach of Vypeen Island, between deserted fisher boats.

"They are looking for prey," Faye says, and points toward the water. "See, the jumping fish over there? That's what they are there for."

She is right, June realizes. Her eyes move from the fish in the water up to the birds in the sky, and back. Don't jump, she wants to say to the fish. Stay hidden. But the fish keep cutting through the surface of the ocean, to sail through the air for a second, before they return to the water again. It doesn't make any sense. Not from her point of view.

Just like the lines Pascal sent. Those lines she had read again and again.

```
so good to here from u. i jst
typed a long msg then it was
b'out  and  it's  all  gone.
while power's away i tried a
sketch of kids in the street
their  kites  in  the  sky.
people  are  difficult  to
figure.

now power's back but i've g0t
class,  but  then  that's  what
i'm here for.

life is strange when u begin
to live.

Thank You
```

Damn blackout. That was the first thing June had thought. Damn blackout that killed the long message for her. The one that she now would never receive. If it had been for her at all. But why else would he mention it?

June gazes out to the water, wondering once more what Pascal had tried to say. He's here for yoga, and won't jump on the next bus to rush to Cochin, but will return to his classes. That was as much as she understood. But why the thank you? And this cryptic line about life being strange, was that about him, or for her?

"Life is strange," June whispers, in another half hearted attempt to brush away Pascal's face from her thoughts. She is here now, with Faye and Nel, on this little island, a ferry ride from Cochin. It's a beautiful day. Seagulls sailing through the sky, silver fish jumping in the water. For a moment, the scene looks harmonic again, as if it all was just a game, as if the birds and the fish were only teasing each other. Then a seagull shoots down, catches another fish and gulps it down.

Alive, June thinks. They swallow them alive. And the fish keep jumping. She shakes her head. "Why are they doing this? Why aren't they hiding?"

"Because they aren't alone out there," Nel says. "There are probably some marlins around, chasing them. That's why they come up to the surface, and try to jump. Or maybe it's dolphins."

June looks at her, surprised.

"Dolphins?"

"You didn't know this? When dolphins hunt schools of fish, they release clouds of bubbles through their blowholes. It's like a net that moves upwards, formed by air," Nel explains, and circles the air with her finger, then draws the finger inward, forming a fist.

The jumping fish aren't teasing. They're trying to flee. "And the seagulls are waiting above," June says and stares at the water surface, suddenly feeling sorry for the trapped fish. "But isn't there a way to escape for them?"

Nel shakes her head. "They would have to cross the bubbles," she says. "And to do that, they would have to change their pattern of behaviour."

"And they won't do that."

"Nope," Nel says.

Faye sighs. "Thinking of it, they are very human in that respect," she says, and cringes when another fish is caught. "This reminds me of a story my yoga teacher back home once told, about the way we all are trapped in our own rooms of life, searching for the door, for the way out of our misery."

June looks at the fish, then at Faye. "And thus...?"

"And thus we walk around in the darkness, until we run into the wall, where we can lay our hands on. So we move along the wall, to find the exit. But each time we are just a step away, we draw the hand back, to scratch an itching spot on our skin, and thus miss the door, again and again."

"How encouraging," June says, and draws a face. "Aren't those stories supposed to end on a somewhat more cheerful note?"

"Maybe this one was supposed to encourage us in our efforts to attend classes."

June puts a finger on the top of her head, on the very spot she had imagined the bowl of glass to stand, the one that would carry her thoughts while she concentrated on her breath moving in… and out.

"Maybe I should try some yoga classes, too," she says. "Learn to sit like a yogi, and to consider all those consequences of all those thoughts, and all those stories."

Then she kneels down, picks up a stone, and throws it into the water in a long haul, so that it bounces on the surface, once, twice, and again, before it finally surrenders to gravity, and sinks towards the invisible ground.

The Key

June stretches her legs and turns from one side to the other. The bed is surprisingly comfortable. Hard, yes, but then that's nothing new. When I get home, I will be able to sleep on the floor, no problem, June thinks. And eat without cutlery. I am really getting better at that.

A smile crosses her face when she remembers the evening, the dinner at the Thali place, where they had talked about the places they could go to next: take the bus to Allopey, and then a backwater boat to Varkala, the beach town set on a cliff.

"Or we could head towards Madurai and Pondicherry," Nel had said, "and visit the Indira Gandhi Wildlife Sanctuary on the way. I asked in the travel agency, there are buses leaving from Cochin to the Sanctuary every day. So it's all up to us."

They had been the only foreigners in the place, and thus, had been the centre of attention again when their meal arrived. And they had done well, there, in front of their plates of dhal and vegetables, the cups of sauces, the staples of fritter. Pretty well.

"You're sure you don't feel like a goodnight drink in the harbour bar?" Faye had asked on their way home.

In response, June had yawned. "You don't really want to see me fall asleep on a table, do you."

She had even considered skipping the shower. But then, her skin was still salty from the daytrip to Vypeen. And sandy. So she had slipped out of her clothes, and had turned on the shower warily. It had been too late for the water to be still warm, but it hadn't been cold either. Probably the last portions of the warm water barrel.

From the shower, she had moved straight into her bed, ready for sleep, all fresh and clean. And to her surprise, awake.

But then, maybe that's what I need at the end of this day, June thinks. Not a drink at the harbour, but some time off for myself. She opens her eyes again, and gazes at the window. No moon there, but a streetlamp, shining yellow, guarding the night, bringing back the memories of the other tale Faye had told there, at the long empty beach of Vypeen Island:

"It's a bit more uplifting than the blind room story," she had said, her voice all serious, yet the sparkle in her eyes tells another truth. "Or to be more precise: it at least includes a journey, and the key to wisdom."

"You know the key to wisdom?" June had asked, not really trying to hide her doubts.

"I know the story about the key to wisdom," Faye had corrected her. And then she had told it, there, in the shade of one of the boats:

"A long time ago, at the beginning of the days, the Gods gathered in the sky, and created the world: air and earth, water and fire, the earth and its continents. Next came the plants and the animals. On the seventh day, they made mankind. Finally there was just one thing to be added: the key to wisdom. They searched for a place, afraid that mankind would find it before they were ready for it. But all the hiding places they considered didn't seem safe enough, neither the highest mountain, nor the deepest sea. So they sat there, probably like we are sitting here now, trying to figure out the ultimate answers."

At this point, one of the seagulls had sailed over their heads, as if it were trying to catch their attention.

"Or maybe it is as curious as we are," June had said, and had watched the seagull sailing away. Then she had turned to Faye again. "So tell now, the key. Where did they hide it?"

Faye had pointed at the horizon, and smiled. "Not there," she had said, and then slowly moved her arm, until her hand pointed first towards Nel, then June, and finally towards herself. "Right there," she had explained. "They hid the key in the heart of men, sure that they will never look for it there. And they were right. Since that day, the years follow each other, while mankind roams the world, searching for the key, unaware that they already have it. That they had it, all the time."

"Right there," June repeats, and suddenly it is present again, this feeling that she had in the plane to Mumbai already, this feeling that the borders that separate the outside from the inside aren't fixed, that they indeed only exist in our minds, solid as long-grown attitudes. And that all it takes to cross them is one weightless move through the shadows of our thoughts, swift like the wings of the night bird that cuts through the lamp light.

June breathes in, and out again. Then she closes her eyes and makes a mental note to remember her dreams, those dreams that were yet to unfold.

~ THE END ~

About & Beyond

Travel Bio

It was in January 2001 that I first travelled to Asia. I had a plane ticket to Bangkok, a brand new backpack filled with too many things, a guidebook, and five weeks of time. "Send e-mails from there," my friends back home said. "And pictures."

So I did, trying to give them an idea of how it feels to be on the road, to travel without the safety net that comes with package tours, with booked hotels and arranged round trips.

It was in Thailand that the idea of going to India took shape. "The thing about India is that it is another world altogether. The most amazing things just happen there. You have to go to see it yourself," another traveller told me, "it's just a flight away."

Just one flight away. Not even half a day in the plane, and you are there. But then, that's true for half of the countries of the world, wherever you live. And the other half, it's only two flights away. All those places to be visited. How could I resist?

Six months later I had the ticket. The plan was to visit Nepal with a friend first, to see the Himalayas, and do some trekking there. From Kathmandu, I wanted to fly to Delhi, and visit Rajasthan. Maybe add a trip to Sri Lanka. But life had it different: in June 2001, the Nepal royal family was massacred by the heir to the throne. A travel warning was issued for Nepal. Shocked by the sudden rise of violence in the region, we decided to change our plans.

Thus, Laos and Vietnam become the next destinations, with the journey starting in Thailand again. In 2002, a trip to Cambodia followed, and then, in January 2003, finally the trip to India. In retrospect, this was probably the better way to expose myself to the entangled chaos and charm of Asia: starting in Thailand, which is easy to travel, offers a lot of comfort to the traveller, and is peaceful by nature, with the state religion being Buddhism. From there, on to Laos, a country that is just opening to tourism again after years of closed borders, and that is as unorganized as it is charming in places, with roads that still wait to be paved, and sights that aren't overrun by visitors yet.

Vietnam was in many ways the counterpart to Laos: clogged cities instead of curved country roads, night trains with barred windows instead of slow boats without railings. At least that was how it felt at the start, until I met up with my German friend, and we went to the ocean, and to the hills, to Halong Bay in the Golf of Tonkin, and to Sapa in the Hoang Lien Mountains, where China is a mere 30 miles away.

Then Cambodia, this place of huge contrasts: the scars of the Khmer Rouge regime, the red dust on the roads, and for the first time, the confrontation with poverty, with children who are raised as beggars, with cripples who depend on coins handed by strangers in the street. And on the other side: the temple complex of Angkor Wat, bigger than the Pyramids of Egypt. A magic place that is filled with artful designs, with ancient tales, with statues and memories. Boats instead of cars, rivers instead of streets. Not many travellers there, compared to Thailand, but the ones you meet seem to have been all around the world already, telling tales from Africa and South America – and India. No matter where I went, I ran into people who started to tell me about India.

"Maybe that is because it is time for you to go there," a woman said to me, putting into words what I already felt. Back home, I started planning the trip, and this time it finally worked out. In January 2003, I boarded the plane to Mumbai. By then, my backpack was battered and my friends got so used to receiving travel mails from Asia in winter that they tended to greet me with: "You're still here?" when they saw me after December had turned to January.

A question that turned to "Have you put together another one of your travel pages?" after I came back from a trip. Those travel pages also marked the move to the world of online words and pictures for me. The first page I created in the internet was a page about Thailand. After that, in an almost yearly rhythm, the pages about Laos and Vietnam, about Cambodia, and about India followed. I started to receive e-mails from people who came across those pages, and looked for advice for their own trip. That's where the idea for this book came from, a travel novel that gives an idea of how it feels to travel through India with a backpack, and that also offers practical advice, inside the story, but also here, in an extra chapter that includes those questions and answers that resulted from my online travel page – and the link to those pages that include pictures, online diaries, flash films, and also maps and a few short stories.

The website that takes you there is:
http://www.blueprint21.de/travel.htm

For more of my words and pictures, visit my homepage:
http://www.blueprint21.de

Enjoy the journeys~~

Dorothee

Travel Tips

PLANNING

When is the best time to go to India?
The thing about India is, it's really is huge, and its regions differ immensely in culture and climate, the way countries in Europe do. If you want to travel to the South, starting in Mumbai, heading to Goa and Kerala, the best time is October to February, when temperatures are moderate (weather in India goes in 3 seasons, they are: cool: October - February, hot: March – June, monsoon: July – September).

Any advice for planning my trip?
Time is the key factor for planning your trip. I would say that three weeks is the minimum for a trip. As a general rule, India, like all of Asia, is enjoyed best by spending more time in fewer places. Make a rough plan for your route before you leave, yet keep your schedule flexible: the best way to travel in India, especially if you have time, is to go with the flow, develop your route as you go, based on the advice of other travellers you meet along the way.

Where can I get first-hand information from other travellers?
One of the best ways to get tips from other travellers are travel boards, like the one on www.lonelyplanet.com – their forum is called the "Thorn Tree," and has a special India section with topics ranging from "What do I really need to bring?" to "Anyone know the train time of that night train from Mumbai to Goa?"

ITINERARIES

What was your exact itinerary for your trip to the South?

plane to Mumbai
2 days in Mumbai
night train to Goa (Margao), shared taxi to Benaulim
3 days in Benaulim
night bus to Hampi
6 days in Hampi
night train to Bangalore
1 day in Bangalore
sightseeing bus to Mysore
3 days in Mysore
night bus to Cochin, ferry to Fort Cochin
3 days in Cochin
public bus to Allopey
1 day in Allopey
backwater boat to Kollam, shared taxi to Varkala
4 days in Varkala
night bus to Margao, shared taxi to Palolem
4 days in Palolem
night train to Mumbai
2 days in Mumbai
plane back home

I can't find Mumbai on my map. Where is it?
On the West Coast, in the middle. Bombay is the old name, Mumbai the new name, but they are both still in use. Just like Allopey is also called Alappuzha. Cochi is also Kochi, and Chennai is also Madras.

Have you visited Rajasthan, too? Where did you go?
Yes, on another trip, but also starting in Mumbai. I had 5 weeks back then, and the route I took was: Mumbai – Udaipur (I spent nearly a week there, palaces, lakes and roof top views) - Jodhpur – Jaisalmer (staying in

the fort, doing a camel safari, sleeping in the desert) – Bikaner – Jaipur -
Agra (Taj Mahal!) - Varanasi (the holy city at the Ganges) - Delhi.

THINGS TO TAKE

What do I need to think of when packing?

Pack light. Take clothes that are easily washed. Go for a walk with your
backpack when it is packed, and then decide if you really need that third
pair of trousers and the second guidebook. Also remember that you can
buy stuff while travelling, so you don't have to bring everything you
think you'll need.

What about documents?

You will need a visa to enter India, so make sure to get this one in time at
the Indian embassy in your country. Make copies of your passport,
drivers license, insurance, visa, plane ticket, emergency credit card
numbers, friends' addresses, etc. and leave one copy at home, take one
copy with you. Also you could scan those documents and e-mail them to
yourself or a friend, in case the documents get lost or stolen.

What items did you take in your medical kit?

I bought a standard first aid kit at a pharmacy. Then I went to the doctor
and updated my Polio, Diphtheria and Tetanus vaccination, and added
Hepatitis A+B and Typhus at the same time. The anti-malarial drug I
took was Doxycyline. Also I took a Vitamin B1 tablet daily, this helps to
keep the mosquitoes at bay as Vitamin B1 changes the scent of skin
slightly.

For updated medical advice, check online travel pages like
www.tripprep.com or www.cdc.gov, as the medication really depends
on the current situation, the season, and your destination. As some
vaccinations need to be given in well advance, and as some of the
potential diseases are quite serious (hepatitis, malaria, rabies), and as the

whole topic is a bit complex, I suggest you make an appointment with your doctor early, at least 6 weeks before you leave.

Backpack or suitcase?

Definitely a backpack. You will come through places that aren't exactly made to wheel a trolley along. Also a backpack is more convenient for climbing stairs or stepping into boats – and it's easier to store it in trains and rickshaws.

What kind of camera did you bring?

I had a rather low price and lightweight camera with me, so that I could carry it around easily, and didn't need to worry about it being stolen.

MONEY

Approximately how much does it cost to travel in India?

Compared to Europe, Australia or the States, the costs of travelling in India are surprisingly moderate. If you plan on staying in mid-range guesthouses that offer comfortable bedrooms with a shower, have decent a breakfast, lunch, and dinner, and also do some sightseeing every day, buy some gifts etc., a budget of about \$20 - 30 per day will cover your expenses.

Is it a good idea to go with a little amount of money in dollars and a credit card?

I would suggest to split the money into cash in US dollars, traveller cheques in US dollars, and your credit card. With this mix you should be fine.

Do I have to worry to find an ATM machine?

ATM machines are standard in all bigger towns. Still it is a good idea to

take some traveller cheques with you, and to always have a $20 and $50
note in a pocket, in case of an emergency.

Where do I store the money?
It's safer and also practical to put it in different places. Wear a money
belt, but also have a purse for paying in shops, restaurants, etc.

STAYING SAFE

Is it safe to travel in India?
Travelling in India is about as safe as travelling in any other country.
However, like everywhere, there are places that may not be very safe for
tourists, especially when travelling late at night. The best way to avoid
dangers is to take the standard precautions:

- Get some information about the places you want to go before you go
there.

- It's always a good idea to let the hotel / guesthouse staff know where
you want to go, and ask for their advice.

- Try not to travel alone at night. If you have to, don't walk, rather take a
taxi.

- Always look like you know where you're going; be confident and in
charge of the situation.

- When something sounds too good to be true, it probably is (like free
taxi rides or cheap jewellery).

I heard from a friends who had a terrible start of their trip to India.
The start of the trip is one of the crucial times: you arrive jetlagged and
without much of a clue how things work, your body isn't used to the
different food, you aren't used to beggars and chaotic traffic, and just

then you have to make dozens of decisions every day, have to establish some kind of routine for handling situations.

To make things a bit easier, give yourself a slow and comfortable start. Book the first hotel ahead, so you can don't have to search for a hotel right after arrival, especially when you arrive in the night. Start in a mid-range hotel, so you have some extra comfort. If possible, do not fly into Delhi, rather start in Mumbai, which probably is the most Western city in India.

Be a bit careful with the food in the beginning, start with easy dishes like rice & vegetables, and try the more curious sounding dishes in the course of time. Make sure you always carry a bottle of drinking water with you, don't risk drinking tap water.

How do I find my ways?
To avoid getting lost, always ask for the destination before getting into a bus / train / boat, and also tell the conductor or another passenger who knows the route where you need to get off, so that you don't miss your stop. Also it's a good idea to take your guesthouse / hotel card with you when you go for a sightseeing walk, so that you can hand the card to the taxi driver and ask him to take you there in case you get lost.

GUEST HOUSES / HOTELS

Do I have to make reservations for the guesthouses?
If you aren't travelling on bank holidays, you should be fine without reservation. And even though it is a bit of a hassle sometimes to go and look for a place to stay after you just arrived from a long bus or train journey, the best way to get a good room is to take some time and shop around once you arrive in a new place, as guesthouse / hotels don't follow an exact 1-star to 5-star ranking system, and even in the same place, rooms can differ significantly

Are there guesthouses / areas you can recommend?
Some of my personal favourites are:

Mumbai – Bentley's Hotel / Colaba area
Hampi – Shanti Huts / across the river
Udaipur – Jheel Guesthouse / room with a lake view, guesthouse with
rooftop terrace
Agra – Hotel Sheela / side street near the East Gate of Taj Mahal
Varanasi – Vishnu Guesthouse / at the Ghats

How do you find a good guesthouse?
Read the guesthouse suggestions on the way to a new place already, and
decide on an area where you want to stay, then choose one or two
guesthouses that sound good by description. When you arrive there,
visit the first place, and if other places are close, then visit those, too,
before you make a decision (ask if it's okay to leave your backpack, so
you don't have to drag it around). Have a look at the rooms, and at the
restaurant. I try to find places that are on side streets, and thus a bit
quieter, have an inviting atmosphere and a place where you can meet the
other guests, or just retreat to when you need a break. Rooftop terraces
are great, just like gardens or courtyards, especially in bigger cities.

GETTING AROUND

Should I travel by bus or stick to trains?
If you have the choice, take the train. It is more comfortable (you can
walk around a bit, buy something to drink / eat, there are toilets, etc.)
and it is safer than travelling on the road. Buses are easier to book,
though, often from one day to the next, whereas you will find that trains
might need to be booked days ahead.

I heard you can book some trains via internet.
That's right. For some train routes, you can get tickets on the internet,
this works quite well – you take the printed booking confirmation with
you, and the train guard will hand you your ticket on the train. The

webpage that offers direct reservations for Mumbai to Goa is
www.konkanrailway.com. Another helpful link is:
www.indianrail.gov.in - an online passenger reservation site providing
schedules, availability, and fares.

Which train tickets should I get?

I would recommend 2nd class AC – that way you are staying in an air
conditioned cabin, and you have a reserved seat. When taking night
trains, I usually try to get the upper berth – so you can retreat to your
berth and are a bit away from the movement on the ground. To get train
tickets, you can either go to the railway station yourself, and stand in line
– or you can buy tickets through travel agencies, or through your
guesthouse / hotel. They charge a small fee, but it saves you time and the
hassle of dealing with opening hours and finding the right building and
counter.

Rickshaws and taxis – any advice for those?

Always agree on the fare before you get into the rickshaw or taxi. Ask
other travellers or guesthouse / hotel stuff about the running rates for
taxi rides.

CULTURE & COMMUNICATION

Do I need to learn Hindi before I go to India?

You will be fine with English, it's one of the official languages in India
(dating back to colonial times). But it is a good idea to know some of the
key words in Hindi:

namaste – hello / goodbye
shukriya – thank you
acha – okay / I understand
koi bat nahi – you are welcome
kshama kijive – excuse me / sorry

ji ha – yes
ji nahi – no

Some other words that are helpful to understand:

ashram – spiritual community
bagh – garden
baksheeh – tip or bribe
banyan – Indian fig tree
chai – tea
curd – yogurt
dhal – lentil dish
ghat – a series of steps that lead to the water
kurma – a mild curry
lassi – yogurt drink
masala – spicy
naan – flat bread
niwas – house
pradesh – state
raj – rule
sadu – a holy man
tandoor – clay oven

How difficult is it to get into conversation with Indians?
Due to English being an official language, and probably also due to the
long history of foreigners travelling through India, it's relatively easy to
get into conversation while manoeuvring through streets, shops, and
temples – for example, I had interesting talks with tour guides, shop
owners, students, travelling families in the train, internet café owners,
artists – and the sister of a bride at a wedding I got invited to
spontaneously in a restaurant in Udaipur. When strangers are unusually
friendly and offer you free rides or free drinks, you should be careful
though, they might be more interested in your purse than in your
personality.

Any Dos and Don'ts I have to think of?

In restaurants: as Indian food is usually eaten with the hands, people will wash their hands before they have their meal. There usually is a sink in the dining room, you will find it when watching the other guests.

This is also useful after having finished your meal.

In temples: take your shoes off before entering a temple.

In any case: Don't get angry and aggressive. Stay cool, whatever happens. Especially stay cool when dealing with officials, policemen, or guards.

Do I really need to bargain?

Yes. That is, if you don't want to pay double the running rates. But don't worry. It only feels strange in the first days, then you get used to it, and also know the procedure: you ask a shop owner / taxi driver / guesthouse owner how much something costs, you get told a price, you offer about half of it, and after a few more takes, you meet somewhere in between. Before starting to bargain, you should have an idea of the prices. Ask other travellers, or ask in your guesthouse what you can expect to pay.

How did you deal with people hassling you?

Ignoring them seems the best way to deal with them. No reply, only a hand gesture that signals that you aren't interested and want to be left alone. But then, they are only doing their job in a way. That's what I told myself when I got annoyed.

What about taking pictures of people?

Some people find it intimidating, some find it funny, some will ask that you send them a copy of the picture, some will ask for money. Photographing can sometimes also be a great way to interact with kids, especially when you have a digital camera and can show them their pictures on the little monitor. Another thing about photos – at several occasions, Indians asked me if they can take pictures with me. It first seemed strange to me, but then, as I also took pictures of people, I thought it is a good way to return the favour.

SINGLE FEMALE TRAVELLERS

I still am a bit concerned about being a woman travelling alone in India.
Basically, if you're female and alone, you attract attention. This doesn't always have to be bad thing – you will get the odd celebrity moment that way, with people following your every move even though you are just a traveller sitting in a restaurant or waiting for the train. Sometimes it leads to interesting conversations, or to invitations to be guest at a wedding.

But to not draw attention of the wrong kind, you have to be aware of the fact that if you're wearing clothes that accentuate your sexuality, it's seen as an invitation. Modest western clothing is fine to wear, though, like jeans and t-shirt or long skirts and blouses.

Some methods to cut down the attention are:

Buy a Salwar kameez, this is a long, loose tunic or dress over baggy pants and sandals. Wearing the common clothes, you won't stand out in the crowd that much, and there's a good chance you will be treated with more respect, simply by looking more respectable. Just don't try to mix Indian and western clothing, this might have the effect of looking silly.

Use a scarf to cover your hair, and sunglasses to avoid eye contact. This also protects you from the intense sunlight.

Take time to find yourself a guesthouse / hotel where you feel comfortable, so you have a place where you can retreat when you feel hassled. Also take time when choosing a restaurant: you don't want to be the only woman sitting there and being stared at.

But again, don't get paranoid. Like everywhere, there will be some idiots, but there also will be some real gentlemen around.

GENERAL ADVICE

What was the best travel advice you were given?
On the first day of my first journey to India, I received a mail from a friend with a couple of practical India tips. This is what he wrote:

1) relax, just think of it all as of a kind of dream

2) as one Indian man told me, "Everything is possible is India, some things just take a little more time."

3) if you are lost or get in trouble look for the man with the turban, he will be tall and bit heavy, with a big black beard and his name will be Mr. Singh. He will help you out.

Any last minute advice?
Take a big dose of humour and patience with you. Don't expect things to go the way you usually would expect them to work. Laugh about things going wrong, and see them as an experience.

CPSIA information can be obtained at www.ICGtesting.com
Printed in the USA
BVOW02s0247311215

431480BV00001B/53/P